T0323996

Cambridge Elements ≡

Elements in Metaphysics
edited by
Tuomas E. Tahko
University of Bristol

MODAL NATURALISM

Science and the Modal Facts

Amanda Bryant
University of Calgary

Alastair Wilson
University of Leeds and Monash University

CAMBRIDGE
UNIVERSITY PRESS

Shaftesbury Road, Cambridge CB2 8EA, United Kingdom

One Liberty Plaza, 20th Floor, New York, NY 10006, USA

477 Williamstown Road, Port Melbourne, VIC 3207, Australia

314–321, 3rd Floor, Plot 3, Splendor Forum, Jasola District Centre,
New Delhi – 110025, India

103 Penang Road, #05–06/07, Visioncrest Commercial, Singapore 238467

Cambridge University Press is part of Cambridge University Press & Assessment,
a department of the University of Cambridge.

We share the University's mission to contribute to society through the pursuit of
education, learning and research at the highest international levels of excellence.

www.cambridge.org
Information on this title: www.cambridge.org/9781009462563

DOI: 10.1017/9781009351645

When citing this work, please include a reference to the DOI 10.1017/9781009351645

First published 2024

A catalogue record for this publication is available from the British Library

ISBN 978-1-009-46256-3 Hardback
ISBN 978-1-009-35163-8 Paperback
ISSN 2633-9862 (online)
ISSN 2633-9854 (print)

Modal Naturalism

Science and the Modal Facts

Elements in Metaphysics

DOI: 10.1017/9781009351645
First published online: December 2024

Amanda Bryant
University of Calgary

Alastair Wilson
University of Leeds and Monash University

Author for correspondence: Alastair Wilson, a.j.j.wilson@leeds.ac.uk

Abstract: How do we know what is possible or impossible, what is inevitable or unattainable, or what would happen under which circumstances? Since modal facts seem distinctively mysterious and difficult to know, the epistemology of modality has historically been fraught with uncertainty and disagreement. The literature has been dominated by rationalist approaches that emphasise a priori reasoning (sometimes including direct intuition of possibility). Only recently have alternative approaches emerged which recognize a broader range of sources of modal knowledge. Yet even emerging non-rationalist views have tended to assign scientific investigation at best a supporting role. Our project in this Element is to develop and defend a new approach to the epistemology of modal facts which assigns a central role to scientific investigation. According to modal naturalism, science (construed broadly) is our primary source of evidence concerning the modal facts.

Keywords: modal naturalism, naturalism, modal epistemology, naturalised modal metaphysics, science and modality

ISBNs: 9781009462563 (HB), 9781009351638 (PB), 9781009351645 (OC)
ISSNs: 2633-9862 (online), 2633-9854 (print)

Contents

1 Introduction

The epistemology of modality is the philosophical study of our knowledge of modal facts. How do we know what is possible or impossible, what is inevitable or unattainable, or what would happen under which circumstances? Since modal facts have often seemed distinctively mysterious and difficult to know, the epistemology of modality has been fraught with uncertainty and disagreement. It has frequently been assumed that, insofar as modal knowledge was possible, its source had to be some form of rational insight because experience tells us only about the actual. The literature has therefore been dominated by rationalist approaches that emphasise a priori reasoning (sometimes including direct intuition of possibility). Only recently have alternative approaches emerged which recognise a broader range of sources of modal knowledge. Yet even emerging non-rationalist views have tended to assign scientific investigation at best a supporting role.

Our project in this Element is to develop and motivate an approach to the epistemology of modal facts which assigns a central role to scientific investigation. According to *modal naturalism*, science (construed broadly) is our primary source of evidence concerning the modal facts. This is a broad programme, with a variety of implementations differing with respect to specific details of the evidential role played by science. In this Element, we will focus on two versions: descriptive modal naturalism and prescriptive modal naturalism, which we distinguish and discuss in the next section. Descriptive modal naturalism focuses on our actual methods for acquiring modal knowledge: it says that scientific investigation in practice plays a central role in modal epistemology, whether or not it is in principle replaceable by a priori investigation. Prescriptive modal naturalism goes further, saying that scientific investigation is indispensable for settling certain important modal questions. Both versions of modal naturalism in turn come in various grades, depending on which questions about modality are viewed as involving scientific input. The result is a varied landscape of modal naturalist views rather than a single monolithic doctrine.

Modal naturalism, as a family of views about the nature of our evidence for modal facts, is an epistemological rather than a metaphysical programme. However, epistemological and metaphysical questions are closely linked: what modal facts there are and what they are like is relevant to how we can best gain knowledge of them. Modal naturalism is, we shall say, an epistemology of the extensional aspects of modal metaphysics. It has close affinities with the programme of 'naturalised metaphysics', which brings the descriptive and explanatory resources of science to bear on metaphysical questions that philosophers traditionally address using a priori methods alone. Modal naturalism has a similar orientation, being antithetical to *purely* a priori modal theorising (although not to a priori reasoning more generally). The aim of this Element is to explore modal naturalism's potential as a full-fledged and distinctive theoretical alternative to standard approaches to modal epistemology – including especially approaches which privilege conceivability, intuition, and other forms of rational insight.

We are primarily interested in the evidential bearing of science on the modal facts themselves, rather than the evidential bearing of science on the way we come to know the modal facts. Some recent work in a broadly modal naturalist tradition has emphasised the contribution cognitive science can make to understanding our processes of imagination and counterfactual evaluation. This approach is exemplified in the work of Daniel Nolan, which we discuss further in Section 7.2. Our main focus, however, is elsewhere: on the direct evidential bearing of scientific discoveries on the modal facts. If cognitive science is relevant to our thesis of modal naturalism, for example, it is relevant in virtue of enabling the acquisition of knowledge about the nature and variety of possible cognitive agents.

How, if at all, can scientific experimentation and theorising bear on modal questions? Some of our motivating examples, set out in Sections 8 and 9, comprise scientific discoveries about the modal status of phenomena of contemporary or historical scientific interest. Science has, we suggest, settled many previously open modal questions. Can life exist without sunlight as a source of energy? (Yes.) Is there an upper limit on the possible mass of a star? (Yes.) Can nuclear fusion of hydrogen into helium be achieved at room temperature and pressure? (No.) Can a spaceship ever overtake a photon? (No.) In addition to these examples, which are posed in technical terms, other cases of potential scientific modal discovery can be identified and puzzled over pre-scientifically. Can life emerge from non-life? (Yes.) Can free human actions be predicted in advance? (Maybe.) Are humans necessarily mortal? (Yes.) How big could an insect become? (At least 70 cm wingspan.) All these questions are about the topography of modal space; they are not wholly about occurrent events in our actual world. In slogan form, modal naturalism holds that science, not isolated rational insight, is our best guide to this modal landscape.

This Element is structured as follows. Section 2 describes the conceptions of modality, naturalism and science with which we will be working; it also discusses the consequences of a broadly naturalistic outlook for the epistemology of modality in particular. Section 3 presents the core of the modal naturalist position and distinguishes some different types and grades of modal naturalism. Sections 4–6 critically discuss alternative general approaches to the epistemology of modality: modal rationalism, modal empiricism, counterfactual accounts. Section 7 discusses in more detail how precisely modal empiricism and other views seemingly in the vicinity of modal naturalism relate to it. We then motivate modal naturalism directly in Sections 8 and 9. Section 10 highlights some more general advantages of modal naturalism over alternative modal epistemologies. Section 11 concludes, reiterating our case for taking modal naturalism seriously and summarising the ways in which proper consideration of the view can reshape the debate over modal epistemology.

2 Modal Inquiry, Naturalism, and Science

2.1 Epistemology of Modality

The epistemology of modality is a highly contested domain. There is no consensus on core questions such as 'does conceivability entail possibility?' Even those who endorse some version of that particular inference (e.g. Chalmers 2002) recognise that the conceivability-based route to modal knowledge is fraught, and subject to restrictions and caveats which limit its applicability. Rivals to conceivability-based approaches include concept-based accounts, which tie modal knowledge to conceptual competence (Section 4); empiricist accounts, which typically assign experience a significant role in the acquisition of modal knowledge (Section 5); and counterfactual-based accounts, which take our procedures for evaluating counterfactual conditionals to be the foundation of modal knowledge (Section 6). We find it striking that none of these views explicitly assign any central role to science in modal epistemology.[1]

The lack of engagement with science in modal epistemology is at odds with a more general movement within metaphysics, and the epistemology associated with that metaphysics, towards an increased role for science and its discoveries. We have seen such shifts in the metaphysics of causation (e.g. Dowe 2000; Andersen 2017), in the metaphysics of time (e.g. Price 1996; Callender 2017), in the metaphysics of laws (e.g. Maudlin 2007; Loewer 2020), in the metaphysics of mind (e.g. Dennett 1992; Drayson 2021) and in the metaphysics of fundamentality (e.g. French 2014; McKenzie 2017). But this shift has not occurred to any appreciable degree within the philosophy of modality.[2] We aim to change that by exploring the prospects for a thoroughly naturalistic modal epistemology.

Modality and science have had a generally uneasy relationship. Empiricists have in various ways hoped to tame modality by regarding it as entirely

---

[1] As we will discuss in Section 7, Williamson (2016) does endorse an account of the modal content of science which is congenial to our favoured modal naturalism. However, we see this as complementary to his broader counterfactual account of modal epistemology – an account that we will suggest underdetermines the naturalistic credentials of particular instances of modal reasoning.

[2] Some exceptions are discussed in Section 3.4; they include Leeds (2007), Ladyman and Ross (2007), and Wilson (2020).

linguistic in origin, to be explained in terms of logical truths and definitions, or as some aspect of our own thinking projected on to the world. Quine was a notorious opponent of modality (Quine 1953a, 1953b); he retained the traditional equation of *de dicto* necessity with analyticity, and thereby rejected it as unclear in light of his influential critique of the analytic/synthetic distinction. In addition, Quine influentially criticised *de re* modality on the grounds that it mistakes a feature of how a thing is picked out for a feature of the thing itself.

Under Quine's influence, some avowed naturalists have considered modality to be simply beyond redemption. Other philosophers with naturalist tendencies have responded to this critique by offering deflationary pragmatist vindications of modal talk which regard modal claims as non-factual in character; van Fraassen (1977) and Thomasson (2020) are examples. These views fall outside the scope of modal naturalism as we intend it. As this Element will make clear, we don't share the Quinean distaste for modality. Regarding Quine's attack on modal notions, we agree with Williamson when he says:

> Since Quine's official methodology involves taking our metaphysics from our best theory of the world, which is supposed to include physics, it is unfortunate for him that our best theory employs something like his bugbear, de re modality. Indeed, any dynamical system validates de re formulas . . . Thus Quine's naturalistic deference to natural science is in tension with his rejection of quantified modal logic. (Williamson 2016, 478–479)

We would add that natural science's employment of modal notions is not incidental: those notions perform crucial explanatory work (Williamson 2016, 474). We discuss this point further in Section 10 as part of our positive case for modal naturalism.

Naturalistic suspicion of modality, rather than flowing from considerations of logic and analyticity, may instead flow from the Humean thought that perception has no modal content. This line of argument can be generalised, from a lack of perceptual access to modal facts to a lack of empirical access more broadly. As Hale puts the point:

> [E]xperience – roughly, sense-perception and introspection, together with what we can infer from their deliverances – leaves us in the dark about what *might* be . . . the interesting question concerns knowledge of *unrealized* possibilities . . . It is precisely because possibilities may go unrealized that experience cannot teach us what must be so. (Hale 2002, 1)

This Humean attitude is inimical to modal naturalism. If experience were no guide to the merely possible or the necessary, then science's prospects for illuminating modal matters would be nil – at least except insofar as science is itself an a priori enterprise. Applying a naturalistic lens to questions of modality would be futile, and modal theorising would have to take the form of *free-range metaphysics* – metaphysics constrained primarily by demands for consistency, simplicity, intuitive plausibility, and explanatory power, while being at best constrained nominally by science (Bryant 2020a). We reject the Humean line of thought; in our view, science can reveal modal facts and, as such, naturalistic modal metaphysics is both possible and desirable. However, we think the Humean line of thought has historically contributed to the dominance of the rationalist view that modal truths can only be known through non-empirical means. We will examine that view in detail in Section 4.

2.2 Modality

One of the core reasons why modal epistemology has often seemed intractable is that the broader metaphysics of modality is deadlocked with no consensus around any single approach, and the competing metaphysical approaches seem to have distinctively different epistemological implications. In contemporary modal metaphysics, one finds linguistic theories of modality, property-based theories, dispositional theories, conventionalist theories, primitivist theories and even various different versions of concrete modal realism. Since theories of the structure of modal space and theories of the content of modal space interact in non-trivial ways, debates about the specific content of modal reality tend to falter unless we adopt some working assumptions about what modality is and how it works.[3] Be that as it may, in this Element, we will aim for neutrality wherever possible on the background theory of modality; we will only assume that modality is a real enough phenomenon for there to be a philosophically significant distinction between the objectively possible and the objectively impossible. This excludes hard-line anti-modality views such as conventionalism (i.e. the view that modal truths are in some sense true by convention) and modal nihilism (i.e. the view that there are no modal truths) but is otherwise, we hope, dialectically benign.

To facilitate neutrality on metaphysical questions, we will distinguish between two components of a complete system of modal metaphysics: the core metaphysics and the extensional metaphysics. The core metaphysics is typically the relatively compact set of definitions and substantive principles that comprise the basic account of some key metaphysical notion, while the extensional metaphysics is the fuller theory which provides descriptive detail of how the basic account plays out in some or all cases. We believe this sort of distinction is fairly widespread, although it goes under different names in different cases. For example,

---

[3] Mallozzi (2021) defends this metaphysics-first approach to the epistemology of modality. See Boardman and Schoonen (2023) for a rejoinder.

Cameron (2012) defends Lewisian modal realism from a critique by Divers and Melia by distinguishing between the modal realist analysis of modality (i.e. a theory of what makes for possibility) and the modal realist theory of what worlds exist (i.e. a theory of what possibilities there are). To take another example, it is standard to distinguish a core aesthetic realist theory of art (i.e. a theory of what it is to be beautiful) from an extensional aesthetic realist account of which particular artworks are beautiful. In each case, the core and extensional metaphysics had better mesh, at pain of instability of the overall account. But the core metaphysics may fall short, perhaps far short, of determining the extensional metaphysics. So it is in the present case. Core theories of modality still tend to leave extensional questions open: saying what a possible world is like does not pin down which particular possible worlds there are. Consequently, we can get some traction in considering the extensional questions directly. Whether modality is grounded in language or in properties or in essences, we can still ask coherently whether it is possible for there to be a unicorn, or a closed timelike curve, or an anyon.

Our metaphysical neutrality has its limits, particularly with respect to the modal status of the fundamental laws of nature. The examples in Sections 8 and 9 fall into two classes. In Section 8, we discuss scientific discoveries of possibility; in Section 9, we discuss scientific discoveries of impossibility. While we think the examples of possibility are compelling regardless of the modal status of the laws of nature, they tend to support only descriptive modal naturalism rather than the more robust prescriptive modal naturalism. The examples of discovery of impossibility, if acknowledged as such, would strengthen the case for prescriptive modal naturalism; however, taking these latter examples seriously requires commitment to the necessity of at least some of the laws of nature. So the overall import of our modal naturalist proposal will depend quite sensitively on whether one believes that the fundamental laws of physics really could have been different. We will return to this point in Sections 3 and 9.

Modal naturalism is intended as a thesis about the epistemology of an objective form of modality, which goes beyond merely nomic possibility, where this is understood as a restriction on some more inclusive notion of possibility.[4] For those who are comfortable with a Kripke-inspired notion of metaphysical modality, it will be simplest to think of this notion as our target – whether metaphysical modality is understood in terms of properties (as by Stalnaker) or in terms of potentialities (as by Vetter) or in terms of essence (as by Fine). But even those sceptical of all these specific conceptions of 'metaphysical modality' can, we think, make sense of modal naturalism. At minimum, what is required for

---

[4] As we explain in Section 3.4, the view that science is our primary guide to nomic modality is common ground in the debate over modality, and so it does not amount to a version of modal naturalism as we use the term.

a version of modal naturalism to be correct is that there be some objective, non-nomically restricted form of possibility to which science is our primary guide.

2.3 Naturalism

Now, on to the 'naturalism' part of our modal naturalism. Naturalism has a variety of forms and modes of application, surveyed for example by Papineau (2020). The term 'naturalism' sometimes has anti-religious and physicalist content, which we set aside as not directly relevant to our concerns. We are interested instead in a strand of naturalism that aligns philosophy with science. As the term is applied within recent metaphysics, naturalistic metaphysics is metaphysics that is robustly constrained by science.[5] This much is agreed on by almost every self–identifying naturalistic metaphysician, but the agreement doesn't extend much further.

Some defenders of naturalistic metaphysics tie it closely to specific metaphysical doctrines like dispositional essentialism (Ellis 2001), anti-Humeanism (Mumford and Tugby 2013) or ontic structural realism (Ladyman and Ross 2007); others see naturalism as a purely metametaphysical doctrine with no direct consequences for first-order metaphysics. And although all naturalistic metaphysicians acknowledge some role for science in metaphysics, they diverge in their thinking about the nature and significance of this role and about whether there remains any distinctive role for the a priori.

In other work (Bryant 2020b; Wilson forthcoming) we have discussed some varieties of naturalism. Rather than attempt a full taxonomy of naturalist views here, we will focus on one variety we find most promising and plausible in connection with modality: an epistemological form of naturalism, which maintains that the content of our best theories in science places distinctive epistemic constraints on the content of theories in metaphysics.[6]

Our epistemological form of naturalism should not be confused with Quine's epistemological naturalism, according to which there is no a priori knowledge or justification; we are willing to grant the coherence of a category of the a priori for the sake of argument. Our preferred form of naturalism also contrasts with metaphysical approaches (which emphasise continuity of subject matter between

---

[5] A terminological note: we will use the terms 'naturalistic' and 'naturalized' interchangeably. Although the term 'naturalized' in Quine's 'Epistemology Naturalized' on the face of it expresses a social metaphor – the absorption of the epistemologist into the community of scientists – the resulting view is itself a version of naturalism by our lights. So both terms are apt for our purposes.

[6] Hence our preferred version of modal naturalism is a relative of what Emery (2023) calls 'content naturalism', as distinguished from 'methodological naturalism'. Content naturalism is the view that '[w]e should not accept metaphysical theories that conflict with the content of our best scientific theories'. Methodological naturalism is the view that '[m]etaphysicians should, whenever possible, use the same methodology that scientists use'.

science and metaphysics; cf. Morganti and Tahko 2017), with methodological approaches (which emphasise similarity of method between philosophy and science, even where these are understood as fundamentally distinct investigations; cf. Paul 2012; Emery 2023),[7] and with toolbox approaches (which hold that metaphysics is valuable just to the extent that it contributes useful tools to science or to philosophy of science; cf. French and McKenzie 2012).

We prefer the epistemological version of naturalism principally because it is robust enough to impose genuine constraints on metaphysical theorising, while still being flexible enough to allow that metaphysical inquiry may address subject matters which are at least partly distinct from scientific subject matters and that metaphysical inquiry may appeal to certain tools or methods which are not directly employed by science. The spirit of our version of modal naturalism is reflected in Callender's claim that '[i]n metaphysics we should take possibilities and necessities only as seriously as the theories that generate them', which should be 'systematic' theories of large domains, 'possessing many theoretical and empirical virtues' (2011, 44). Mature scientific theories best fit the bill.

We have said that modal naturalism requires that science epistemically constrains the extensional aspects of modal metaphysics. Bryant (2021) expands on this notion of theoretical constraint and argues for its epistemic significance. Roughly, a theoretical constraint is a limit on the contents that can be admitted into a theory. For instance, we often expect our theories to be adequate to the data, internally consistent, unificatory, or virtuous in certain ways (simple, elegant, fruitful, etc.); holding such criteria fixed limits the sorts of contents that are admissible into the theory. As these examples suggest, theoretical constraints often admit of degree, trade off against one another, and can be assigned different weights in different contexts, according to one's aims. A metaphysics robustly constrained by science is one where science plays a prominent role in guiding what goes into the theory; that is to say it forecloses certain theoretical avenues or options (by being inconsistent with or otherwise incongruent with them) and pushes the inquirer toward others (by being consistent with and evidentially supporting them).

In some cases, including those discussed in Sections 8 and 9, the modal implications of scientific discoveries may be reasonably specific. This doesn't mean that metaphysics is always clearly settled by science, or easily derivable from it; on the contrary, naturalised metaphysics typically faces significant underdetermination of theory by evidence. Making a robust naturalistic case for a metaphysical claim requires difficult and contentious interpretation and

---

[7] Although our epistemological naturalism is distinct from methodological naturalism, it nevertheless has methodological consequences – namely, that modal epistemologists should give consideration to scientific evidence.

conceptual regimentation of the scientific theories involved – and any such case remains hostage to empirical fortune. Still, after suitable reflection, we might reasonably conclude that some scientific theory fits much more naturally with some metaphysical views than others. Epistemic constraints arising from science can in this way reduce, although not eliminate, metaphysical underdetermination and disagreement.

Modal naturalism, as we have characterised it here, is compatible with both 'uniformist' and 'non-uniformist' views of modal epistemology – views which allow one or multiple paths to modal knowledge (see Wirling 2020 for this distinction). Modal naturalists might say that science is our best route to modal knowledge, but that there exist other routes which are less useful to us for whatever reasons; alternatively, they might say that science is our only route to modal knowledge. This distinction is not directly aligned with our distinction between descriptive and prescriptive forms of modal naturalism: a uniformist version of modal naturalism does entail prescriptive modal naturalism, but both prescriptive modal naturalism and descriptive modal naturalism remain compatible with non-uniformism about modal knowledge. Uniformist modal naturalism is an interesting and radical view, but it is not obligatory for modal naturalists and we will not be arguing for it in this Element.

2.4 Science

Since epistemological naturalists like ourselves make scientific results central to the evidence base for modal inquiry, we immediately face the problem of characterising science. The 'demarcation problem' is a perennial one: the nature of science has proven immensely difficult to elucidate precisely. In laying out modal naturalism as an approach to modal epistemology, we need not commit to a single, definitive response to the demarcation problem; in principle, a wide range of characterisations of science can be combined with modal naturalism. In the abstract, modal naturalism remains neutral on the nature and boundaries of science, and, as such, individual naturalists are welcome to bring their preferred conceptions of science to the modal naturalist framework and to explore the consequences.

We prefer a conception of science according to which the boundaries of science are vague and the differences between scientific and non-scientific ways of knowing are often a matter of degree rather than kind (Haack 2003; Williamson 2007; Chakravartty 2017). One consequence of considering 'science' a vague concept is that what counts as *naturalised* modal theory inherits a corresponding degree of vagueness. We take this to be a feature rather than a bug. We will also assume a broad and inclusive conception of the individual sciences, which is not limited to fundamental physics but includes the natural sciences more broadly, social science, and mathematics. However, to avoid complications arising from disagreement about how to understand social science and mathematics, the majority of our examples in Sections 8 and 9 will be drawn from natural science.

We may use the institutions of science as a rough proxy for the collection of reliable methods and sources of evidence associated with science. However, we acknowledge that not all work conducted within the institution of science is epistemically adequate or optimal, and we grant, conversely, that some activities occurring outside the usual institutional contexts might share some of the positive epistemic features of science (see e.g. Hansson 2019 on experiments conducted by farmers). These qualifications should make clear that modal naturalism does not impose any requirement that a society discover, for example, classical mechanics, before its members can justifiably form any modal beliefs.

While, for convenience, we identify paradigm examples of science by appeal to the social institution, what does the heavy lifting in our account is science understood as an epistemological phenomenon, which pre-dates and extends beyond institutional boundaries. Clearly, our ostensive reference via institutions doesn't settle the deeper issue of which particular features of science are epistemically significant and responsible for its sustained explanatory and predictive success. Candidate features include systematicity, empirical exposure, controlled experimentation, and self-correction – but again, in the abstract, modal naturalism remains neutral here.

2.5 Summary

In this section, we described the prevailing disagreement regarding foundational conceptual matters in modal epistemology and modal metaphysics, and we declared our intended neutrality on most of those contested matters. We also distinguished between core modal metaphysics and extensional modal metaphysics, where core modal metaphysics concerns foundational concepts and principles, and extensional modal metaphysics concerns particular modal facts. We suggested that a fruitful mode of inquiry takes a bottom-up approach and considers the extensional questions as directly as possible. However, we acknowledged that the import of the cases we will consider later in the Element depends on the view taken of higher-level matters such as the modal status of the laws of nature. We described the sense of 'naturalism' at work: an epistemological form, according to which our best science places epistemic constraints on extensional modal metaphysics. In other words, scientific evidence disconfirms certain modal claims and supports others. We then discussed our broad conception of science, for which we take the institutions of science to provide an adequate proxy.

3 Modal Naturalism

3.1 The Core View

Modal naturalism, as we use the term, is the view that science is central to the fulfilment of our epistemic aims (knowledge, justification, or whatever else they may be) with respect to the modal facts. This view does not presuppose any specific account of the metaphysics of modality: in principle, one can combine modal naturalism with views of the nature of modality as different as Lewisian modal realism, Stalnakerian actualism, or Siderian conventionalism. Some of these accounts of modal metaphysics may themselves be more or less naturalistic; see Section 3.4 and Wilson (forthcoming) for discussion. But for present purposes, modal naturalism is purely a thesis about the role of science in the epistemology of modality. It says that science has a key role in the achievement of our epistemic aims via-à-vis the modal facts, by providing evidence which bears on them.

We set aside modal eliminativism (the view that modal discourse is incoherent or otherwise vacuous), fatalism (the view that only the actual is possible) and conventionalism (the view that the distinction between the possible and the impossible is wholly conventional) for the purposes of this discussion; our argument is directed at philosophers who take modality seriously but who are unsure how modal facts can be evidentially grounded in the deliverances of science. We take it that any metaphysical framework that gives a substantial role to modality (which, in practice, includes almost every metaphysical framework that is taken seriously today) requires supplementation by at least a minimal story about the epistemology of modality.[8] Specific theories of the nature of modality, then, will only play a role in our discussion insofar as they constrain possible accounts of the epistemology of modality.

Although there are various types of modal claims one could focus on, we simplify here by focusing on the epistemology of questions about what is and is not possible. From a realist point of view and adopting for simplicity a possible-worlds framing, this reduces our domain to questions about the extension of modal reality: what are the possibilities? We will adopt this worlds-based framing in what follows, and accordingly we will talk of different theories concerning the modal facts as different hypotheses concerning which possible worlds there are. However, we think that our argument can be straightforwardly adapted to theories which assign no central role to possible worlds: even anti-realists about possible worlds will need to capture the difference between more and less inclusive conceptions of what can happen.

---

[8] An adequate framework should, in our view, also address the question of the function of modal judgement (Divers 2009), but we will not focus on that here.

A core tenet of modal naturalism is that science bears evidentially on modal matters. Here we operate with a broad sense of 'evidence', such that any information which bears on rational degree of belief counts as evidence. In Bayesian terms, for science to evidentially bear on modal claims is simply for the rational posterior probability of the modal claim, conditional on some scientific evidence, to be different from the unconditional probability of the modal claim.[9] This formulation immediately runs into complications, though, given the usual idealisation of Bayesian epistemology that non-contingent propositions all have rational probability 1 or 0.[10] We mention the Bayesian formulation mainly to give a sense of how direct an epistemic connection between scientific evidence and modal judgement we have in mind.

The most obvious way for science to bear on modal matters (since the actual is possible) is for our conception of the range of objective possibilities to be expanded by learning from scientific evidence that a scenario not previously justifiably regarded as an objective possibility is in fact actual. This has, we think, happened numerous times in the history of science. But our conception of the range of possibilities can be expanded by science in other ways, and we will discuss some such cases in Section 8. At any rate, the idea that science bears on modal inquiry by expanding our view of the range of possibilities is just one among several conceptions of what science can do for us in modal theorising – conceptions we will explore further in Section 3.4.

Modal naturalism, put in terms of knowledge, says that our primary and best evidence for modal claims is to be found in the body of knowledge obtained through our best science. This formulation of the thesis is congenial to a view of science such as that of Bird (2022), according to which science consists in the accumulation of scientific knowledge. However, versions of the modal naturalist thesis can readily be formulated in the context of other accounts of scientific epistemology which focus instead on more internalist forms of justification.

Our 'first-order' modal naturalism, a view about how we know the modal facts, leaves open a second-order question about how we know modal naturalism itself: is the evidence taken to support first-order modal naturalism *itself* scientific (giving us second-order naturalism) or a priori (giving us second-order non-naturalism)? A potential regress lurks in the background here.

---

[9] We will assume that there are some objective constraints on rational priors, but subjectivist approaches can instead regard the different brands of naturalism as associated with different choices of priors.

[10] Generalising Bayesian epistemology to non-contingent subject matters, including mathematics and metaphysics, remains a major challenge. We cannot address it in detail here; see Titelbaum (2013) for discussion.

We remain neutral on the second-order question for the most part;[11] our focus will be on defending first-order modal naturalism. However, it is worth noting that, since we will motivate modal naturalism using concrete scientific examples, our argumentative approach will be at least partly second-order naturalistic.

3.2 Descriptive versus Prescriptive Modal Naturalism

In this section, we distinguish two distinct forms of modal naturalism, descriptive and prescriptive, which differ in their relative permissiveness regarding the potential for a priori routes to modal knowledge. Descriptive modal naturalism is a (perhaps contingent) methodological claim about how we human investigators in practice typically acquire and justify our modal knowledge. Prescriptive modal naturalism is a (probably non-contingent) claim about what sources of evidence can in principle enable the acquisition and justification of modal knowledge.

Prescriptive modal naturalism involves denying that the modal facts can be known purely a priori, while descriptive naturalism does not. It is compatible with descriptive modal naturalism that there be purely a priori routes to all the modal facts, so long as we typically can't – or don't – make use of these purely a priori routes and instead have to justify our actual modal beliefs with additional forms of evidence. In contrast, according to prescriptive modal naturalism, no fully a priori route to the acquisition and justification of all modal knowledge is available, even in principle. On the prescriptive approach, the modal subject matter is such that at least some modal knowledge cannot be gained purely a priori: in that case, scientific evidence is indispensable to the acquisition and justification of our modal beliefs.

We think that descriptive modal naturalism is plausible on grounds that are largely independent of the underlying metaphysics of modality. Whether or not the fundamental laws of nature are contingent need not bear on how we actually come to most of our modal beliefs. By contrast, the plausibility of prescriptive modal naturalism is tightly linked to the character of the modal facts. If the fundamental laws of nature are entirely contingent, such that there is a background space of metaphysically possible worlds with different fundamental laws, then it looks like science will play no role in providing evidence about that background modal space. Accordingly, while our presentation of descriptive modal naturalism in 3.3.1 will be theory-independent, our presentation of prescriptive modal naturalism in Section 3.3.2 will be more theory-dependent.

---

[11] For a view of modality which is naturalistic at both first and second orders, see Wilson (2020); see also the discussion of grade 4 metaphysical modal naturalism in Section 3.3.

Different approaches to the metaphysics of modality will provide the basis for increasingly strong forms of prescriptive modal naturalism.

3.2.1 Descriptive Modal Naturalism

Descriptive modal naturalism is 'descriptive' to the extent that it concerns the realm of actual modal epistemic practice and what is or is not expedient therein. Unlike the prescriptive modal naturalist, the descriptive modal naturalist doesn't conclusively rule out purely a priori pathways to modal knowledge. Rather, she allows that, for all we know, the modal facts could in principle be knowable purely a priori by ideal reasoners or knowers quite unlike us.

For comparison, consider a population of creatures which, in virtue of limits to their cognitive capacities, cannot prove mathematical facts for themselves, but which nevertheless can acquire justified mathematical beliefs through reading textbooks written by more advanced creatures. In this scenario, mathematics remains an a priori discipline because it is in principle possible to justify mathematical beliefs a priori, even though the creatures in question gain all their mathematical knowledge a posteriori.[12] Descriptive modal naturalism allows that we might be in a comparable situation, for all we know, vis-à-vis the modal facts.

But the descriptive modal naturalist is not concerned, in the first instance, with this sort of science-fiction scenario. She sets aside in principle knowability and ideal or alien agents. She reasons: *who knows* whether we might in principle come to know about modal matters purely a priori, and how could we possibly determine what an ideal or alien agent could know a priori? If the descriptive modal naturalist is motivated by broader naturalist proclivities, she might even find such talk inherently suspect. Science can only demonstrate so much about the hard 'in-principle' limits on knowability (for minds like or unlike ours) and the normatively loaded matter of ideal reasoning. Instead, the descriptive modal naturalist is interested in practically efficacious pathways to modal knowledge for epistemic agents with cognitive capacities like ours, in epistemic circumstances suitably like our own. She recognises that those capacities and circumstances are largely contingent. She looks at the historical successes and failures of modal reasoning, such as those we will discuss in Sections 8 and 9, and concludes that unchecked a priori speculation demonstrably isn't a good guide to the modal facts – while science demonstrably is. According to the descriptive modal naturalist, a sound modal epistemology takes *that* as its starting point.

---

[12] Burge (1993) argues that the status of beliefs as a priori is preserved over testimony; for the sake of this example, we suppose with Malmgren (2006) that testimony does not preserve a priori status.

We have said that descriptive modal naturalism is compatible with any view of the modal status of the fundamental physical laws. That's because the reliability of how we come to know the modal facts in the particular way or ways we do appears to be independent of whether or not the fundamental physical laws could have been different.[13] Still, suppose that the descriptive naturalist happens to be a *contingentist* – that is, she happens to think that the fundamental physical laws are not metaphysically necessary. This contingentism has important implications for her brand of descriptive modal naturalism. In particular, coupling descriptive modal naturalism with contingentism entails that we have no direct path to knowledge of metaphysical necessities. The contingentist can't simply point to the laws of physics and get metaphysical necessities for free, as can her *necessitarian* counterpart (i.e. her counterpart who believes the fundamental physical laws *are* metaphysically necessary). When science tells us, for example, that nothing can travel faster than light, contingentism entails that it has acquainted us with a *mere* physical necessity. For the contingentist modal naturalist, science can inform us of metaphysical necessities only indirectly, in virtue of logical inferences from the possibilities of which science does inform us. When science teaches us, for instance, that it is possible for spacetime to be curved, we learn via deductive inference that it is not impossible for spacetime to be curved. Coupling descriptive modal naturalism with contingentism therefore results in relatively thin knowledge of the domain of metaphysical necessity. By contrast, if necessitarianism is held fixed, the modal naturalist can decisively rule out any 'in principle' a priori pathways to modal knowledge and have greater purchase on the domain of metaphysical necessity.

3.2.2 Prescriptive Modal Naturalism

Prescriptive modal naturalism is a thesis about our modal knowledge, not a thesis about the modal facts. But what modal facts there are determines what modal knowledge can be knowledge of, and what modal facts are like helps determine the ways we can come to know them. So, modal epistemology is not wholly isolated from broader considerations concerning modality. In particular, the modal status of the laws of nature bears on what sorts of modal conclusions can be drawn from empirical investigations of various sorts.

Certain precursors of the modal naturalist epistemology have associated it with a hardline 'modal necessitarian' metaphysics, according to which the fundamental laws of nature are the same at every possible world (see e.g. Edgington 2004; Bird 2007; Wilson 2013). As we noted in the previous section, this metaphysics is optional for defenders of descriptive modal naturalism. But

---

[13] This assumption is sometimes rejected; see Wilson (2013).

must prescriptive modal naturalists be modal necessitarians? Modal necessitarianism does tend to support prescriptive modal naturalism: if the actual fundamental laws of nature constrain the entire range of genuine possibilities, and if it is primarily by doing science that we acquire evidence about the fundamental laws of nature, then science has a central role to play in modal epistemology. Indeed, if there are no further constraints on the genuine possibilities beyond those imposed by the fundamental laws of nature, then modal naturalism follows immediately. Prescriptive modal naturalism and modal necessitarianism thus form a potentially attractive package, which one of us has defended elsewhere in the specific context of Everettian quantum theory (Wilson 2020).

More moderate views of the modal status of laws are available, which also align with prescriptive modal naturalism. Certain general symmetry or conservation principles are intuitively 'less contingent' than the specific force laws which respect those general principles (Lange 2009). The interpretive distinctions typically drawn in philosophy of physics between boundary conditions (including initial conditions), dynamical laws, and 'constants of nature' make room for some of these to be metaphysically necessary and others metaphysically contingent (Wolff 2013; Linnemann 2020). Even if only certain general or structural aspects of the actual physical laws were metaphysically necessary, science would retain an indispensable role in coming to know those necessities.

We have distinguished between two forms of modal naturalism, descriptive modal naturalism and prescriptive modal naturalism, which differ in their attitude toward the in-principle availability of purely a priori paths to modal knowledge. For the purpose of evaluating modal naturalism, we aim to stay as neutral as possible on the modal status of the laws of nature. Although the metaphysical necessity of the fundamental laws (or of suitable aspects of the fundamental laws) would seem to enforce prescriptive modal naturalism, we also think that a strong case for descriptive modal naturalism can be made regardless of whether the fundamental laws of nature could have been different.

In our overall case for modal naturalism, we presuppose neither the truth nor the falsity of necessitarianism. However, some of our examples will only count in favour of modal naturalism in the context of modal necessitarianism. Accordingly, we divide our core motivating examples into two categories: discoveries of possibility (Section 8) and discoveries of impossibility (Section 9). Our cases of discoveries of possibility can support modal naturalism regardless of the modal status of the laws of nature. Our cases of discoveries of impossibility, however, tend to support modal naturalism only if the fundamental laws of nature are non-contingent; contingentists about the fundamental laws can explain away these examples as discoveries concerning 'mere' nomic impossibilities.

3.3 How Exclusively Does Science Bear on Modality?

There are multiple dimensions along which one can distinguish varying strengths of modal naturalism. One such dimension – the focus of this section – concerns how large an overall contribution science makes to meeting our modal epistemic aims. That is to say, there are differing conceptions of just how significant scientific evidence is to modal inquiry as compared with other potential sources of evidence.

In this sense, a relatively weak view of the relevance of science to modal inquiry holds that *some* of the evidence bearing on modal claims (in practice or in principle) is scientific evidence. Essentially, the claim is that science has some relevance to modal inquiry. Such a view is consistent with modal rationalism, modal empiricism, and counterfactual accounts, so it is not by itself characteristic of modal naturalism. As we will discuss in Sections 4–6, modal rationalism holds that modal knowledge is gained primarily a priori, modal empiricism holds that it is sometimes or often gained a posteriori, and counterfactual accounts hold that it is gained through counterfactual reasoning. The view that some evidence bearing on modal claims is scientific is consistent with these frameworks, because it says only that appeal to scientific evidence is one way to meet our epistemic aims. Such a view allows that pure a priori justification, a posteriori justification outside the context of science, or counterfactual reasoning outside the context of science might also conduce to those aims, and in fact might be what most often guides us in practice.

A stronger view holds that science has special evidential import relative to the modal facts. On this view, science is not just one source of evidence about the modal facts among others but our *primary* source, in virtue of the especially strong evidence it generates. Such an account is inconsistent with modal rationalism, since it assigns evidential primacy to science and not to unsupplemented a priori reasoning. The view remains potentially reconcilable with modal empiricism and counterfactual accounts, at least to the extent that a posteriori evidence and counterfactual reasoning are important components of science. However, it does suggest that extant versions of modal empiricism and counterfactual accounts leave out an important part of the overall picture.

Finally, an even stronger view holds that all evidence bearing (in practice or in principle) on modal claims is scientific evidence. That is, science is the only source of evidence regarding the modal facts. We referred to this view in the previous section as uniformist modal naturalism; we might also call it *exclusive modal naturalism*. Exclusive modal naturalism is inconsistent with standard modal epistemologies. If systematic science is the only way to meet our epistemic aims with respect to modality, then neither pure a priori reasoning, nor empirical observation, nor counterfactual reasoning alone are sufficient in that regard; rather, there must be something distinctive about the package of scientific practices that makes science a unique conduit to modal knowledge (or justification or understanding, etc.).[14]

Many will find exclusive modal naturalism unpalatably strong. It is hard to know what the identifiable and *sui generis* aspects of science would be that would make it *the one and only* conduit to modal knowledge (or whatever other epistemic accomplishments). Moreover, would-be proponents of the view would need to argue that no non-scientific evidence bears on modal judgements, which would be a significant dialectical burden. Alternatively, one might think that logic and/or mathematics impose evidential constraints on modal judgements which are not properly regarded as scientific constraints. It has been argued that a priori philosophical components of modal epistemology are required in addition to all the evidence science can offer (e.g. Morganti and Tahko 2017); we shall have more to say about this view in Section 7.3.

For the time being, we aim to stay as neutral as possible regarding how much of the evidence bearing on modal facts is scientific; our aim in this section is just to lay out the range of different positions that fall under the rubric of modal naturalism.

3.4 How Extensively Does Science Bear on Modality?

In the previous section, we focused on how exclusively scientific evidence bears on modal questions; in this section we focus instead on how extensively science shapes our knowledge of different sorts of modal facts. Some views claim that scientific evidence is relevant only to a constrained subset of the modal facts; other views extend the relevance of scientific evidence across the whole range of modal facts. In short: some metaphysical views are more deeply naturalistic than others.

With a nod to Quine's three grades of modal involvement (Quine 1953b) – in which Quine distinguished three increasingly more committal attitudes one might take to modal discourse – we will classify naturalistic approaches to objective modality into several categories, depending on the depth of scientific modal relevance they allow. Each grade views science as bearing on a broader set of modal facts than the previous grade.

The first category of views we will distinguish – in order to set them aside – is not a version of modal naturalism at all:

- **Ungraded:** There is no such thing as objective modality.

---

[14] This would make modal naturalism inconsistent with accounts such that of Biggs (2011), which indexes modal knowledge to one isolated tool of science, namely abduction.

According to ungraded views, scientific discoveries are in principle irrelevant to the nature and extension of nomological and metaphysical modality. Modal truths, insofar as there are any, are conventional. Views of this sort have been defended by van Fraassen (1977), Cameron (2010), and Thomasson (2020). Because they deny any objective standard of correctness for judgements of possibility and necessity, and since we are assuming a broad metaphysical realism about our modal subject matter, these approaches fall wholly outside of our classification of approaches to modal epistemology.

Although the next category of views incorporates realism about objective modality, they are still not versions of modal naturalism as we understand it.

- **Grade 0**: Scientific evidence has no evidential bearing on objective possibility.

According to grade 0 views, nomological possibility is compatibility with the laws of nature, and science (obviously!) bears on what the laws of nature are – but it does not bear on any broader form of objective modality. This sort of view is held by a variety of philosophers (including Armstrong 1983, Bealer 1987, and Lowe 1998 – note that the latter two authors are canonical modal rationalists of the kind we will discuss in Section 4).

At grade 0, science can tell us about the physical modal facts. However, this does not fall within the scope of the version of modal naturalism which we endorse in this Element. Our version of modal naturalism concerns objective modality and scientific input thereinto. At grade 0, the background space of objective possibility remains completely isolated from scientific evidence; hence we set it aside.

Grade 1 is the first grade that, for our purposes, counts as genuine modal naturalism. It allows scientific evidence to support the acknowledgement of previously unrecognised possibilities.

- **Grade 1:** Scientific evidence can support expanding our view of the objective possibilities.

Philosophers at grade 1 allow that science can reveal objective possibilities, while isolated a priori reflection does not (and, perhaps, cannot). Lewis, for example, claimed to be willing in principle to recognise the possibility of 'unHumean whatnots' in light of quantum theory (Lewis 1986). A more familiar case is the recognition of the possibility of curved spacetimes in light of general relativity. These cases, and others like them, are discussed in detail in Section 8.

Grade 1 is the version of modal naturalism that finds widest support in the existing literature. To move beyond it requires accepting that science can provide evidence that something a priori coherent is nevertheless impossible. Such a move generally requires an account of modality according to which there are objective necessities going beyond logical truths or matters of individual identity. The most prominent such approach is contemporary *dispositional essentialism* or *scientific essentialism,* associated with authors like Shoemaker (1980), Swoyer (1982), Ellis (2001) and Bird (2001, 2007). On such views, natural kinds have modally rich characters which are essential to them, so that – for example – salt might necessarily dissolve in water or like charges might necessarily repel. Thus we obtain grade 2 modal naturalism:

- **Grade 2**: Scientific evidence can support contracting our view of the objective possibilities.

Philosophers at grade 2, such as Ellis, make much of the ability of their view to account for science as discovering a genuinely modally rich world. However, it is not clear that the substance of their view fully lives up to this rhetoric. Grade 2 views still typically acknowledge the objective possibility of 'alien' fundamental properties with 'alien' laws, so that there is a possible but uninstantiated property of 'schmarge' which is just like charge except that like schmarges attract (or schmattract). This suggests that grade 2 might not end up being significantly more naturalistic than grade 1: grade 2 views might amount to a mere redescription of grade 1 views, recognising the same general patterns of possible behaviour and differing only over whether natural kinds have their behavioural profiles essentially. To put this challenge in slogan form: at grade 2, scientific discoveries bear on what cannot happen only by bearing on which properties are rightly called by which names.

Concerns over the substantiveness of grade 2 modal naturalism may be addressed by moving to grade 3, which incorporates grade 2 but adds that science can rule out structural possibilities concerning possible patterns of property behaviour. There might, for instance, turn out to be no possibilities with more than eleven spacetime dimensions – not just because any more complicated structural possibilities would not deserve the name spacetime, but because there just are no such structural possibilities.

- **Grade 3**: Scientific evidence can support contracting our view of the structure of the objective possibilities.

As we interpret them, views of this grade are expressed by Edgington (2004), Leeds (2007), Ladyman and Ross (2007), Wilson (2013) and French (2014). The kinds of cases which we ourselves take to best motivate grade 3 versions of modal naturalism are discussed in Section 9.

When it comes to surveying the modal facts – the main modal epistemological project with which we are concerned in this Element – grade 3 is the form of modal naturalism that assigns science the deepest role. However, there is a grade worth mentioning which goes deeper still:

- **Grade 4**: Scientific evidence bears on what objective possibilities are.

Grade 4 extends the bearing of scientific evidence from what we have called the extensional aspects of modal metaphysics to the core aspects of modal metaphysics – that is, to the constitution of modal reality itself. At grade 4, science bears not just on what is possible but on what possibility is.

Grade 4 views are few and far between and best illustrated by example. Wilson (2020) argues that many-worlds quantum theory can be understood as an account of the nature of metaphysical modality. The core proposal of Wilson's quantum modal realism is that metaphysical contingency is variation across different branches of the quantum wavefunction of the universe. The following two principles underpin the quantum modal realist account of modality:

- **Alignment**: To be a metaphysically possible world is to be an Everett world.
- **Indexicality-of-Actuality**: Each Everett world is actual according to its own inhabitants and only according to its own inhabitants.

Beyond quantum modal realism, it is hard to find unambiguous examples of grade 4 views. Certain views which might be described as radical modal naturalism, such as Price's projectivist approach (which we will discuss in Section 7.4), are more naturally classified as ungraded views. Ontic structural realists (Ladyman & Ross 2007; French 2014) also sometimes say things which suggest a grade 4 view: for example, that laws and symmetries are fundamental or constitute modal structure. Insofar as Priest (1987) intends the recognition of contradictions to be motivated scientifically (e.g. via considerations of quantum theory), his dialetheism may also qualify as a grade 4 view. However, there are few discussions of modality in the literature which explicitly commit to the distinctive thesis of grade 4: that the underlying nature of modality is revealed by science in the same way that science reveals the underlying nature of material phenomena.

To summarise the grades again:

- Ungraded: We can know a priori that there is no such thing as objective modality. (Van Fraassen; Cameron; Thomasson)
- Grade 0: Scientific evidence bears on what is nomologically possible. (Armstrong; Bealer; Lowe)
- Grade 1: Scientific evidence expands our view of the metaphysically possible. (Einstein/Minkowski)
- Grade 2: Scientific evidence contracts our view of the metaphysically possible. (Shoemaker; Ellis; Bird)

- Grade 3: Scientific evidence contracts our view of the structure of the metaphysically possible. (Edgington; Leeds; Ladyman & Ross; French)
- Grade 4: Scientific evidence bears on what metaphysical possibilities are. (Wilson; Priest)

For the purposes of motivating modal naturalism, we will focus on grades 1, 2 and 3 in the remainder of this Element. In particular, we will focus in Section 8 on cases from the history of science which can be taken to support grade 1, and in Section 9 on cases which can be taken to support grades 2 and/or 3. We do not regard ungraded and grade 0 views as meaningfully more naturalistic than other mainstream approaches to the epistemology of the modal facts. By contrast, grade 4 is a radical form of modal naturalism; we prefer to focus here on more modest versions of modal naturalism. Since grade 4 plausibly implies grades 1–3, however, we take it that providing a defence of grades 1–3 also lends grade 4 a little indirect support.

3.5 Summary

In this section, we began by setting out some of our framing assumptions, including our focus on questions pertaining to possibility and our minimal realism about modality. We distinguished between descriptive and prescriptive forms of modal naturalism, the former of which assigns science a critical role in how we actually acquire modal knowledge, and the latter of which claims science is in principle indispensable to acquiring modal knowledge. On our characterisation, descriptive modal naturalism decisively rules out a priori pathways to modal knowledge, while prescriptive modal naturalism does not. We distinguished between different conceptions of how exclusively science bears on modal facts, and we discussed the compatibility of those conceptions with standard modal epistemologies. We then distinguished several grades of modal naturalism which differed with respect to the types of modal question that science can help us adjudicate.

4 Modal Rationalism

4.1 Varieties of Modal Rationalism

In this section and the ones that immediately follow, we begin to situate modal naturalism in the broader theoretical context. We start with the most historically dominant kind of view and the furthest from our own: modal rationalism. In Sections 5 and 6, we move on to consider more recent *non-rationalisms* that appear closer in spirit to modal naturalism. In Section 7, we discuss the precise relationships between modal naturalism and apparently nearby kinds of view.

Modal rationalism is the view that knowledge of modal truth is gained primarily a priori. Modal rationalists have proposed two main candidates for the a priori mode of access to modal truths: conceivability and understanding. Conceivability accounts aim to capture the Humean maxim that 'whatever the mind clearly conceives, includes the idea of possible existence, or in other words, that nothing we imagine is absolutely impossible' (Hume 2000/1739, 1.2.8). Some think conceivability entails possibility. For instance, in Chalmers' view, if some statement S is conceivable in a certain way (we may omit the details for present purposes), then there is a metaphysically possible world that satisfies S when considered as actual (2002). Others think that conceivability evidences rather than entails modal truth (Yablo 1993; Menzies 1998). Further, some conceivability accounts are non-epistemic in the sense that they are not concerned with actual knowers in actual circumstances, but with ideal conceivers (Chalmers 2002; Geirsson 2005). In contrast, epistemic conceivability accounts posit conditions for knowers to have modal knowledge in actual epistemic circumstances (Yablo 1993; Worley 2003). On such views, 'whether or not something is conceivable for a thinker depends on what the thinker knows or believes, or what concepts or modes of presentation he [or she] has available or is using to think about the situation' (Worley 2003, 17).

According to Yablo (1993), 'what is conceivable is typically possible, and . . . p's conceivability justifies one in believing that possibly p' (1993, 13). He explains, 'Just as someone who perceives that p enjoys the appearance that p is true, whoever finds p conceivable enjoys something worth describing as the appearance that it is possible' (1993, 5). On this view, p is conceivable for me if 'I can imagine a world that I take to verify p' (1993, 29). While Yablo grants that conceivability is a fallible guide to possibility, he maintains that it is justificatory: 'probably, if my evidence holds, then so does my conclusion' (Yablo 1993, 17). Yablo's claim is not that conceivability is the best guide to possibility, but rather that it is the only guide: 'if there is a seriously alternative basis for possibility theses, philosophers have not discovered it' (1993, 2). The maxim that conceivability is a guide to possibility is, he thinks, 'entrenched, perhaps even indispensable' (1993, 2).

Chalmers (1996) provides a well-known example of what conceivability-based modal rationalism looks like in modal metaphysical practice. He asks us to consider the logical possibility of zombies, which are physically identical to regular human beings but have no conscious experience. He says that the logical possibility of zombies 'seems . . . obvious' (1996, 96). He argues:

> While this is probably empirically impossible, it certainly seems that a coherent situation is described; I can discern no contradiction in the description. In some ways an assertion of this logical possibility comes down to a brute intuition . . . Almost everybody, it seems to me, is capable of conceiving of this possibility. (1996, 96)

In Chalmers' view, the conceivability of zombies entails their logical possibility. Chalmers also argues that 'the metaphysically possible worlds *are* just the logically possible worlds' (our emphasis, 1996, 38). Assuming 'are just' is symmetric (see Rayo 2013 on the symmetry of the 'just-is' operator), the conceivability of zombies entails their logical possibility, which entails their metaphysical possibility. So here we have a conceivability argument for the metaphysical possibility of zombies.[15]

As for understanding-based forms of modal rationalism, there are several varieties. For instance, according to Peacocke (1999), modal knowledge requires understanding modal notions, which carries with it implicit knowledge of the principles of possibility. In his view, modal knowledge consists in the proper use of those implicitly known principles (1999, 162). Likewise, Bealer (2002) gives an account according to which modal knowledge is a function of the determinate understanding of concepts. A subject *determinately* understands a concept if and only if she has 'natural propositional attitudes toward propositions that have that concept as a constituent content' (2002, 102) and 'does not do this with misunderstanding or incomplete understanding or merely by virtue of satisfying our attribution practices or in any other such manner' (2002, 102). Determinate understanding of concepts, together with good cognitive conditions (such as intelligence), yields truth-tracking modal intuitions. If a subject's intuitions were not truth-tracking, 'the right thing to say would be that either [she] does not really understand one or more of the concepts involved, or her cognitive conditions are not really good' (2002, 103).

Bealer gives the following example: suppose that to be a multigon is to be 'a closed, straight-sided plane figure', and suppose that a person in good cognitive conditions determinately understands the concept MULTIGON (2002, 103). Her determinate understanding of the concept generates her truth-tracking intuition that 'it is possible for a triangle or a rectangle to be a multigon' (2002, 103). Similarly, consider the example of water's essential nature. According to Bealer, we get from a posteriori knowledge of the chemical composition of actual samples of water to the modal conclusion that 'necessarily, water = H_2O' by relying on intuitions about hypothetical cases, such as Putnam's twin earth thought experiment, which in turn derive from appropriate concept possession. Possessing the concept WATER gives rise to the intuition that substance XYZ on Putnam's Twin Earth is not water, which gives rise to the modal knowledge that the chemical composition of water is essential to it.

---

[15] This argument is considerably extended and nuanced in Chalmers' later work, but we focus for simplicity on his original formulation.

4.2 The Problem of Intuitions and Other Challenges

Modal rationalists of both the conceivability and understanding ilks often assign a prominent evidential role to intuitions, frequently invoking the language of intuition.[16] For instance, in disambiguating conceptions of conceivability, Chalmers says that one promising form of conceivability, *positive* conceivability, involves imagining or having 'a positive intuition' of a certain configuration of objects and properties within a world, satisfying a certain description (2002, 151). Peacocke suggests that pretheoretic intuitions can support the necessity of certain modal principles (1999, 152–153). Bealer claims that conceptual competence yields truth-tracking modal intuitions (Bealer 2002, 103), even contending that 'it would be unreasonable to deny the evidential force of modal intuition and, in turn, unreasonable to deny that … your modal intuitions are a (fallible) guide to modal truth' (2002, 75).

Plenty of philosophers – including Bryant (2020a), Kriegel (2013), and Ladyman and Ross (2007) – have argued against the evidential value of intuitions more generally. Some evidence from experimental philosophy suggests that at least some philosophical intuitions vary across cultures (Weinberg et al. 2001; Nichols et al. 2003; Machery et al. 2004; Beebe and Undercoffer 2016; Li et al. 2018), and some are vulnerable to certain forms of cognitive bias, such as framing and priming (Wheatley and Haidt 2005; Swain et al. 2008; Schwitzgebel and Cushman 2012; Andow 2016).[17]

It's important to note, however, that the term 'intuition' is used in a variety of non-equivalent ways. So, it is likely that not all the modal rationalists cited have the same thing in mind. A complete assessment of intuition-talk and the associated epistemic practices of modal rationalists would need to disambiguate and approach each usage on its own terms. While we do not have space for such an extended discussion here, and while we recognise that theoretical accounts of intuitions diverge, we think the term refers specifically enough that we can say some general things about it. Let's think of intuitions as neutrally as possible – as whatever it is (thoughts, judgements, feelings, beliefs, dispositions, assumptions, etc.) that thought experiments and other prototypical philosophical methods are testing for.

At least some paradigmatic examples of modal intuition have a poor track record when it comes to acquainting us with metaphysical truths. Ladyman and

---

[16] One exception is Tahko (2017).

[17] However, we acknowledge concerns regarding the methodology of experimental philosophy generally (Kauppinen 2007; Cullen 2010; Woolfolk 2013) and regarding the initial cross-cultural study by Machery et al. (Deutsch 2009; Martí 2009; Devitt 2011; Sytsma and Livengood 2011; Ichikawa et al. 2012). We also acknowledge that results concerning cultural variability have been mixed (Lam 2010; Knobe 2019).

Ross point out, 'science, especially physics, has shown us that the universe is very strange to our inherited conception of what it is like' (2007, 10). For instance, prior to various scientific and mathematical developments, 'metaphysicians confidently pronounced that non-Euclidean geometry is impossible as a model of physical space, that it is impossible that there not be deterministic causation, that non-absolute time is impossible, and so on' (2007, 16). So, the course of scientific discovery has overturned some particularly strong modal intuitions. In fact, science regularly frustrates common sense metaphysical intuitions (Shtulman and Harrington 2016). One might even think that counter-intuitiveness is characteristic of scientific discovery, since surprise is a measure of scientific success (see French and Murphy 2023). At any rate, we believe there is little reason to take intuitions to be even defeasibly evidential in the first place – which is to say, we think defenders of intuitions bear a special burden to show why we should take them seriously at all.

The point is not just that these sorts of modal intuition are fallible, but that some of our strongest modal intuitions keep getting overturned by science. And why shouldn't they? As Callender points out, modal intuitions are 'historically conditioned', not pure and timeless rational insight (Callender 2011, 44). At any rate, if it is indeed epistemically undesirable to assign an unrestrained evidential role to modal intuitions, and if there are viable modal epistemologies that do not, then we should prefer them.

A further reason for thinking that reliance on intuition is a theoretical cost is that it generates brute, intractable disagreement. Modal rationalism is particularly prone to disagreements that bottom out in the dull thud of clashing intuitions. Indeed, Chalmers' zombie thought experiment stands out as a particularly clear example. When we get these brute disagreements, 'the faith that there is anything genuinely at issue can indeed become strained' (Yablo 1993, 38). Unless we find some grounds for rejecting the opposing view, it seems the only option is 'to insist on there being 'facts of the matter' that only oneself and one's coreligionists are privy to', which generates 'something of a credibility problem' (1993, 38). If we are to believe that there is a domain of objective modal facts that we can debate and discover, then modal disagreement should not be brute. Rather, there should be some way of gaining traction on our disagreements.[18]

Reliance on intuition is also a theoretical cost because it makes modal error difficult to identify and account for. Yablo points out, '[m]odal error is a fact of life, and although perceptual error is too, our firmer grip on its aetiology allows

---

[18] For further discussion of this problem, see Fischer (2015); for attempts to grapple with modal dispute and contradiction, see Sidelle (2010) and Thomasson (2020).

us to feel less the helpless victim than in the modal case' (1993, 32). Those teachers who have asked students to conceive of a square circle will likely have had mixed results. Inevitably, some students claim they can do it. Presumably, many of us would say those students are mistaken. Yet it is difficult to explain why. Worse, when we move to other examples, such as those concerning swampmen, zombies, and the like, it becomes far less clear what the answer should be. By contrast, compare perception. We can usually assume that perceptual appearances are more-or-less accurate, because '[m]isperception is something that we know how to guard against, detect when it occurs, and explain away as arising out of determinate cognitive lapses' (Yablo 1993, 32). Modal intuition is not comparable. In many cases, we have no good way of identifying spurious modal intuitions and no good account of them. Clear-cut cases like the square circle are the exception, not the rule. Yablo concludes, '[u]ntil our imaginative excesses are brought under something *like* the epistemological control we have in other areas, we modalize with right, perhaps, but without conviction' (1993, 33). We suggest, by contrast, that modal rationalists modalise with conviction but without right. Truly satisfactory modal epistemologies should be able to account in a natural way for modal error.

4.3 Summary

In this section, we described two prominent forms of modal rationalism: conceivability- and understanding-based accounts. The former regard the cognitive capacity of *conceiving* as the key to modal knowledge; the latter hold that modal knowledge is rooted in adequate understanding of modal notions. We pointed out that modal rationalists of both stripes often explicitly assign a prominent evidential role to intuitions. We suggested that the poor historical track record of prototypical examples of modal intuition casts doubt on the evidential value of at least some forms of modal intuition. We also considered Yablo's points that rationalist approaches generate brute disagreement and have limited traction on modal error.

From the discussion in this section, we can synthesise a (non-exhaustive) list of desiderata for a satisfactory modal epistemology. Such an epistemology should: (1) limit the role of intuitions (or, at least, dubious forms of intuition), (2) have relatively great traction on disagreement, and (3) have the resources to identify and account for modal error. We will suggest in Section 10 that modal naturalism satisfies these desiderata more fully than rival frameworks. In the next sections (Sections 5–7), we will examine recent alternatives to standard rationalist epistemologies of modality (non-rationalist modal epistemologies) and consider their costs and benefits, as well as their proximity to modal naturalism.

5 Modal Empiricism

5.1 Modal Empiricism and Modal Naturalism

Modal empiricism is a relatively recent addition to the modal epistemological landscape (see Fischer and Leon 2017). For our purposes, *modal empiricism* will describe any view that assigns experience a significant role in the acquisition of modal knowledge. Such views come in varying strengths: modest versions say that *some* modal truths are known a posteriori (note that this is compatible with modal rationalism; see for instance Roca-Royes 2007), while the stronger versions say that *many* of them are (Bueno and Shalkowski 2014). Later in this section and in the next, we will consider in more detail how modal empiricism relates to modal naturalism.

Prima facie motivations for modal empiricism include the following. First, as Williamson points out, 'actuality is often the best argument for possibility' (2007, 164). That is because actuality entails possibility according to the widely accepted T axiom of modal logic: if pigs actually oink, then it is possible that pigs oink. However, the actualised possibilities are generally thought to constitute only a fraction of the total set of possibilities. So this motivation does not get us far; it only motivates empiricism about a small subset of modal truths.

A further prima facie motivation is that we discover modal facts empirically. Take Kripke's famous examples of a posteriori essences and identities: water is H_2O, gold is atomic number 79, Hesperus is Phosphorus (1980). We discovered these essences and identities empirically, or so the empiricist story goes. However, while most modal rationalists acknowledge the role of a posteriori evidence in our discovering these necessities, they argue that the modal force of this evidence is known a priori (Tahko 2017; Mallozzi et al. 2023, §2.3). Although science acquaints us with the relevant properties, modal rationalists deny that it acquaints us with their modal profiles; that is, science does not reveal that the properties are essential or that numerical identities are metaphysically necessary. If so, then knowledge of such modal facts requires rational insight. Thus, these prima facie motivating cases do not seem to adequately motivate modal empiricism. A better motivation for modal empiricism would show that the specifically modal content of some propositions is known empirically.

5.2 Varieties of Modal Empiricism

Several modal empiricists aim to show just that. Hanrahan argues for a version of modal empiricism that hinges on the following analogy: 'the imagination is to the possible as perception is to the actual' (2009, 282). That is, imagination fallibly justifies beliefs about what is possible. In her view, imagination is to be understood in a Humean fashion:

[T]he images produced by our imagination are constructed in some way out of elements of what we have previously perceived. So ... the images produced by the imagination could have been produced through the workings (standard or otherwise) of our sensory faculties. (Hanrahan 2009, 293)

This view is empiricist to the extent that it takes imagination to be dependent on and derivative of experience. Hanrahan gives the following example. While cooking, 'a series of images came to me ... of Walter accidentally slicing through one of his fingers ... and they were for the imagination quite forceful and vivacious' (2009, 292). The imaginative experience justifies belief that the proposition *Walter has cut off one of his fingers* is possibly true (2009, 292). According to this empiricist account, our guide to possibility is imagination, understood as an a posteriori form of evidence.

Alternatively, Jenkins (2010) argues that conceivability is a guide to modal truth, but that conceivability should be understood as a function of empirically gained conceptual competence. Jenkins explains, 'the senses may ground modal knowledge by providing ... epistemic grounding for our concepts, which concepts (help to) determine what we can and cannot conceive of, which in turn guides our modal beliefs' (2010, 255). This account is reminiscent of the conceivability-based rationalist accounts discussed in the previous section, except in its claim that the limits of conceivability are at least partly empirically determined.

Accounts such as these face the challenge of clearly distinguishing themselves from traditional rationalist accounts. One potential concern is that reconceiving erstwhile a priori mental capacities – such as imagination and conception – in empirical terms may result in a modal epistemology that differs only cosmetically from rationalist predecessors. A sceptic might say that while a bit of conceptual footwork might allow us to call such epistemologies 'empiricist', in practice they end up mirroring standard rationalist accounts and invoking modal intuitions in an equally problematic way.

Other empiricist frameworks promise to provide more robustly empirical explanations of modal knowledge. For instance, Roca-Royes (2017) provides a similarity-based account of *de re* possibility knowledge about concrete entities. In her view, we come to know about some entity's unrealised possibilities by extrapolating from knowledge of another entity's realised possibilities (2017, 233). For the inference to work, the objects must be relevantly similar, that is, similar in 'categorical intrinsic character' (2017, 233).

Two forms of background knowledge enable such inferences: categorical and nomic. Categorical knowledge is knowledge of the shared features of a class of entities. For instance, knowledge that *animals with hearts can die of heart attacks* is categorical (2017, 230). Such knowledge can derive from

many sources. Sometimes it is straightforward perceptual knowledge.
Sometimes it is 'delivered by a team of epistemic tools including memory,
induction, testimony, abduction, or entitlements of some sort; as illustrated by
our knowledge of quarks, hands, the blackness of ravens, etc.' (2017, 229).
Next, a bridge is needed to get us from a recognised similarity between two
objects and relevant categorical knowledge to a modal conclusion. Nomic
knowledge provides that bridge. Nomic knowledge is the knowledge that
'causal *powers* and effect *susceptibility* depend on qualitative character', or,
roughly, that like causes have like effects (original emphasis, 2017, 229). Such
knowledge enables the extrapolation step, in which we take experience of one
object and draw modal conclusions about a similar object.

Roca-Royes' similarity-based account is compatible with modal naturalism
and can complement it. However, we see modal naturalism as broader in
scope. It will become clear in later sections that we think modal naturalism
can account for a wide range of modal knowledge, not just *de re* possibilities
for concrete objects (though, as we have already said, its precise scope varies
depending on how the naturalist views the modal status of the physical laws).
We will discuss the proximity of the similarity-based account to modal
naturalism further in Section 7.

Some philosophers distinguish between ordinary and extraordinary modal
claims, where (roughly) the ordinary claims concern everyday objects and
scenarios or similar ones, while the extraordinary claims concern unusual
objects and scenarios very unlike the everyday ones.[19] While Roca-Royes
intends her framework to account for ordinary modal claims, other modal
empiricisms attempt to account for extraordinary ones. Fischer develops
a theory-based modal epistemology that rejects any special faculty of modal
intuition and instead leverages our best ways of knowing about the actual
world to account for how we could justifiably believe some extraordinary
modal claims (Fischer 2016, 2017). According to his view, 'we are justified in
believing any interesting modal claim *p* if and only if (a) we justifiably believe
a theory according to which *p* is true, (b) we believe *p* on the basis of that
theory, and (c) we have no defeaters for the belief that *p*' (2017, 8). Fischer
adopts a semantic view of theories that regards them as families of models
representing a system (2017, 19). So, if a model or family of models contains
certain modal commitments, 'then your reasons to believe the theory are
reasons to believe the modal claim' (2017, 22). The account does not presume
that we will always have some justifiably believed theory that speaks to the

---

[19] See Bueno and Shalkowski (2014), Fischer (2016), Mallozzi et al. (2023), Roca-Royes (2018),
and van Inwagen (1998).

extraordinary modal claims we are interested in – and when we don't, 'we should just admit our ignorance' (2017, 14).

We think indexing modal knowledge to our systematic ways of knowing about the world and their outputs is promising. Indeed, that is an important part of the motivation for modal naturalism, as we signalled in Section 2 when we cited Callender's claim that we should take modal claims only as seriously as the systemic theories that generate them (2011, 44). However, it is important for views such as this to spell out the conditions theories must meet in order to qualify as sources of modal knowledge. Fischer claims that it is not just any old theories that can ground modal knowledge; rather, when it comes to justifying extraordinary modal claims, 'we should start looking to our best theories for guidance' (Fischer 2017, 14). This raises crucial questions: Which sorts of theory count as our best theories, and in virtue of what are they best? Without clear answers to these questions, theory-based views are from our perspective incomplete, and may potentially be too permissive. In Section 7, we will discuss in greater detail the relation of Fischer's view to modal naturalism.

A further class of empiricist modal epistemologies – namely, perceptual accounts – make empirically tractable claims about our capacities. For instance, Strohminger argues that sense perception acquaints us with many non-actual possibilities, so that 'I see that I can reach the mug', 'I see that I can climb the tree', and 'I see that I can catch the ball' (Strohminger 2015, 367). She argues, furthermore, that perception acquaints us with necessities; if I reason for long enough that a glass and mug are two different things, '[e]ventually I can just see that it is necessary that the glass is not the mug' (2015, 369). Claims such as this about the contents of perception are amenable to empirical vindication.

Indeed, this sort of view is only as strong as the empirical case for modally loaded perceptual content. How strong is this case? We regard this as an interesting open question, which we will address in the following sections. It merits consideration not only for its relevance to the credibility of perception-based modal epistemologies, but also because it bears on the assumption we used to frame this Element and which has framed so much of the history of modal epistemology: that experience only tells us about the actual. If perception were modally loaded, it would mean the historical dominance of modal rationalism was premised on a mistake. We will draw the same conclusion on independent grounds in later sections. Our canvas of the available evidence in subsequent sections will show that further empirical support is needed for the hypothesis that perception has modal content.

5.3 The Theory of Affordances

Gibson's theory of affordances, a canonical theoretical framework in ecological psychology, approaches the perception-based account.[20] According to Gibson, aspects of an animal's environment – such as 'terrain, shelters, water, fire, objects, tools, other animals, and human displays' (Gibson 1979, 127) – afford certain things to the animal. The affordances of the environment are what the environment 'offers the animal, what it provides or furnishes, either for good or ill' (Gibson 1979, 127). These affordances are modally loaded:

> If a terrestrial surface is [horizontal, flat, extended, and rigid], then the surface *affords support* ... It is stand-on-able, permitting an upright posture for quadrupeds and bipeds. It is therefore walk-on-able and run-over-able. It is not sink-into-able like a surface of water or a swamp, that is, not for heavy terrestrial animals. (Gibson 1979, 127)

Note that the relevant modal properties include both positive properties ('stand-on-ability') and negative ones ('not sink-into-able'). The important point for our purposes is that Gibson believes affordances are perceived:

> If a surface is horizontal, flat, extended, rigid, and knee-high relative to a perceiver, it can in fact be sat upon. If it can be discriminated as having just these properties, it should *look* sit-on-able. If it does, the affordance is perceived visually. (Gibson 1979, 128)

So what is the view, exactly? When we look at an everyday object, do we see everything we could do with it? This would be prima facie implausible, since – as Gibson himself notes – objects afford an 'astonishing variety of behaviours' (1979, 133). A more plausible view would comparatively restrict the contents of the perception, perhaps with reference to some domain of practical possibility encompassing prototypical actions, that is, the kinds of actions routinely undertaken in the course of an animal's everyday life. A rational reconstruction of the view would then be as follows:

> Certain salient surface properties *constitute* certain practical possibilities, so that when we see those properties, we see the relevant possibilities.[21]

---

[20] We thank Jorge Morales for drawing this to our attention.

[21] This is a good deal more finessed than what Gibson says in Ch. 8 of his *Ecological Approach to Visual Perception* (the culmination of his work on the subject). He does entertain the idea that constitution is the right metaphysical lynchpin, since he says, '[p]erhaps the composition and layout of surfaces *constitute* what they afford' (original emphasis, 1979, 124). However, he doesn't explicitly restrict the relevant domains of observed properties or perceived possibilities. He also says that 'what we perceive when we look at objects are their affordances, not their qualities' (1979, 134), which suggests that affordances are perceived directly, not in virtue of the perception of the relevant properties. This is puzzling given previously quoted material, in which

Whether one finds such a view plausible depends on whether one is willing to accept that physical properties *constitute* non-actual possibilities (as opposed to, say, providing a dependence or explanatory basis for them). This is a substantive question about the metaphysics of modality, and in accordance with our aim of neutrality on core modal metaphysics, we will not pursue the matter any further here. However, in principle, we see no reason why an account in which non-actual possibilities are directly constituted by actual physical properties – and thereby are rendered directly perceivable – could not be naturalistically acceptable.

At any rate, the theory of affordances has provided a fruitful conceptual framework for thinking about intelligent, goal-directed behaviour in concrete environments, which has been used in various areas of cognitive science, communication research, information systems, design, human-computer interaction, artificial intelligence, and robotics. Philosophers and scientists have worked to clarify Gibson's account (Turvey et al. 1981; Scarantino 2003); to spell out its ontology (Chemero 2003; Stoffregen 2003; Caiani 2014; Heras-Escribano 2019); to model the perception of affordances (Berhard et al. 2013); to distinguish the relevant perceptual objects, contents, and mechanisms (Sloman 1996; Siegel 2014); and to determine an appropriate methodology for its study (Fromm et al. 2020).

A complicating factor is that, while the language of affordances has been theoretically fertile, its distinctive roster of terms is not defined or used consistently across the sciences or even within individual sciences (Evans et al. 2016; Fromm et al. 2020). On the contrary, discussions of affordances are remarkably disunified. At any rate, notwithstanding the fruitfulness of Gibson's theory qua research programme, it is important to consider whether and to what extent its perceptual claims are supported by empirical evidence.

5.4 The Empirical Status of the Theory of Affordances

Caiani (2014) considers whether the empirical evidence available from cognitive science is compatible with the theory of affordances, understood as the view that we directly perceive motor information about what objects afford (2014, 278). He argues that the evidence suggests a close neural connection between certain kinds of perception and action. Early in the perceptual process, visual stimuli with salient action-related properties (such as graspability) directly activate sensorimotor areas (such as the premotor cortex) functionally involved in the execution of relevant actions, thereby priming the relevant

---

he says that certain discriminable properties (perhaps) constitute affordances and that having certain such properties is a condition of the affordance being visually apparent.

systems for action.[22] According to Caiani, this evidence suggests that the perceptual system picks up motor information about action-potentials directly, without intermediate inference.

While the evidence that certain kinds of perception prime us to undertake certain kinds of action may accord with aspects of the theory of affordances, it is insufficient to establish the hypothesis that we perceive possibilities. This reflects the fact that the alleged perceivability of affordances is just one separable aspect of the theory of affordances (Scarantino 2003). At any rate, that we perceive the graspability of a mug is just one among many possible explanations of why the motor system immediately and automatically prepares to grasp the mug.

For instance, prior experience might have created a strong association between mugs and grasping, which cognitively penetrates perception of the mug. Alternatively, the mug might be immediately, intramodularly categorised as graspable in perception, without any need for seeing possibilities (Mandelbaum 2018). Or perhaps certain non-modal properties of the mug – not its graspability but the structural physical features on which its graspability partly depends (other features being its relation to the would-be grasper, as well as features of the grasper herself) – are the true cause of the relevant neurophysiological changes and the true object of perception.

To be clear, the challenge is not just *that* there are alternate explanations available (a challenge which many or most accounts of available evidence face) but rather that the evidence does not clearly support the hypothesis that we perceive possibilities any more than it supports those alternatives. Perhaps some argument could show that the hypothesis is a better explanation in some respects. Lacking such an argument, the perception-action connection in the brain does not adequately motivate the hypothesis that we perceive possibilities.

An alternative line of argument for Gibson's hypothesis that affordances are perceived might be that the hypothesis fits well within an evolutionary frame-work. For instance, Withagen and van Wermeskerken argue:

> [T]he idea that animals perceive their environments primarily in terms of affordances is very attractive from an evolutionary perspective. After all, in order to survive and reproduce it is of primary importance that animals perceive what affords eating, locomotion, danger, and so on. Hence, it is quite likely that animals should evolve so as to perceive the action possibilities in their environments. (Withagen and van Wermeskerken 2010, 490)

---

[22] On objects automatically potentiating certain motor responses even in the absence of an intention to act, see also Anderson et al. (2002), Craighero et al. (1996), Grèzes and Decety (2002), and Tucker and Ellis (1998).

Yet these sorts of general appeal to evolutionary theory are notoriously problematic.[23] It is easy to say that some capacity or faculty would have been adaptive in an early evolutionary environment, and, as such, sweeping evolutionary explanations are too easily available to be strongly evidential. Since none of the evidence we have considered on behalf of the theory of affordances strongly confirms the hypothesis that we perceive possibilities, let us set aside the theory of affordances.

5.5 New Experimental Evidence for Perceived Possibilities?

While the representation of possibility by human perceptual systems has not yet received much direct empirical study, some recent empirical evidence has been taken to suggest that we sometimes see possibilities. In particular, some experimental results have been taken to suggest that representations of possibility arise in automatic visual processing, prior to higher-level cognition.

In one study (Guan and Firestone 2020), the authors presented subjects with Tetris-like shapes of three general kinds: (1) square, (2) disconnected parts composable into a square, and (3) disconnected parts not composable into a square. When instructed to identify squares, subjects false-alarmed more frequently when shown disconnected parts that could compose a square versus those that could not. Subjects were also faster to identify complete squares when previous trials showed an image with parts that could combine to create a square versus when previous trials showed an image with parts that could not.

According to Guan and Firestone, 'This initial result suggests that, at least for a moment, subjects represented the disconnected parts in terms of the complete object they could create, such that they mistakenly responded that a merely potential object was physically present on the display.' (Guan and Firestone 2020, 4). Further experiments that varied rotation, alignment, and shape had similar results. According to the authors, the results establish 'the robustness and reliability of the visual system's representation of possibility' (2020, 6). Another series of experiments found that 'displays with combinable pieces were perceived as less numerous than displays with non-combinable pieces – as if the mind treated two geometrically compatible pieces as being the single object they could create.' (2020, abstract).

These results are interesting and important. However, their import for modal epistemology remains an open question. The conclusion that subjects saw non-actual possibilities is a philosophically loaded interpretation of the results. Suppose for the sake of argument that subjects did see the possible square that

---

[23] Take, for instance, the many and varied critiques of evolutionary psychology, such as Buller (2012), Kaplan (2002), and Panksepp and Panksepp (2000).

the shapes in front of them could compose. If so, then perception has modal content. Even so, before we become card-carrying modal empiricists, important questions remain. First, the speed of subjects' responses allowed experimenters to say that the possible square was seen, not judged to be there.[24] The possibility was represented in the visual system before the visual information was sent to higher cognition. But since vision was in fact misrepresenting what was presented to the subject, the misrepresentation would have been corrected before long. This raises the question: are all (supposed) perceptions of possibility so fleeting? Do we have the sort of stable, dependable conscious access to them that would be required for perception to be a source of modal knowledge?

Moreover, just how modally laden is perception? How often do our perceptual systems represent non-actual possibilities, and which kinds of possibilities – beyond possible compositions of geometric shapes – do they represent? Geometric composability is one thing; seeing that I can reach the mug or climb the tree is another. In the one case, two shapes that are presented to my visual system are represented as one shape; in the other, the visual system is alleged to be doing much more than simply smooshing shapes together. Whether the visual system represents possible complex actions or sequences of events in addition to shapes is an open question. Putting all this together, we conclude that the empirical evidence does not currently substantiate perceptual accounts of modal empiricism.

5.6 The Distinctness of Modal Empiricism and Modal Naturalism

Having surveyed various kinds of modal empiricism, it may be difficult to see precisely what distinguishes this family of views from the modal naturalist family. Both approaches are typically motivated by dissatisfaction with traditional rationalist frameworks. Moreover, the sciences privileged by the naturalist are bound up with some of the empirical forms of evidence privileged by empiricists. However, while empiricisms and naturalisms are sometimes conflated, modal empiricism and modal naturalism as we conceive them are distinct programmes.

Modal naturalism is defined in terms of science – including all its theoretical components – rather than directly in terms of the empirical. The distinction between the scientific and the empirical is often ignored. Yet it is worth recognising that science goes beyond the empirical, and the empirical goes beyond science. For instance, Chakravartty explains, 'not all sciences actually

---

[24] Strohminger describes some putative pieces of perceptual knowledge as judgements (2015, 367), but judgement is often regarded as post-perceptual. If so, then if we literally see non-actual possibilities, the seeing has to occur before cognitive processes like judgement kick in.

make novel predictions (evolutionary biology), or employ experiments (string theory), or are successful in manipulating things (cosmology)' (2013, 34). As Bryant (2022) points out, scientists implement a range of methods that might be considered a priori, including thought experiments (Galileo's falling bodies, Einstein's train); computability theory, modal logic, and category theory (computer science); and even pure armchair speculation.[25] So, science plausibly includes some elements typically associated with the a priori.

Moreover, the empirical outstrips the scientific. Looking around and acquiring perceptual information about one's surroundings is paradigmatically empirical, but it would only count as science on conceptions much more permissive than our own. Believers in qualia typically regard them as empirically accessible, but qualia are not described by science as we know it. So, to the extent that modal empiricism does not essentially involve science, while modal naturalism does, they are distinct positions. We will speak more to the precise relationship between modal empiricism and modal naturalism in Section 7.

5.7 Summary

In this section, we surveyed some varieties of modal empiricism, including those that characterise imagination and conceivability in empirical terms, the similarity-based account, the theory-based account, as well as accounts that ground modal knowledge in perception. The first sort of view may risk mirroring modal rationalism in significant epistemological and methodological respects. Similarity- and theory- based accounts are potentially complementary to modal naturalism but, as we will explain further in the next section, not themselves forms of modal naturalism. Regarding perceptual accounts, we suggested that the alleged modal content of perception remains to be vindicated empirically. The claim that we perceive possibilities aligns with Gibson's theory of affordances, but we saw that there is not presently a strong empirical case for the perceptual claims of the theory. While recent experimental evidence suggests that subjects may perceive merely possible shapes, it is not clear that the claimed modal content of perception is sufficiently stable, accessible, or complex to constitute a robust pathway to modal knowledge.

---

[25] It should be clear, therefore, that we do not rest our claim that modal naturalism has advantages over modal rationalism on a simple caricature of science, according to which science is wholly a posteriori. On the contrary, it is plausible to recognise some a priori elements of scientific practice, at least insofar as the a priori/a posteriori distinction makes sense at all. The epistemically significant difference between modal rationalism and modal naturalism, then, is that the one relies on *isolated* a priori reasoning while the other – to the extent that it engages with science – does not. In scientific contexts, a priori reasoning operates in concert with other methods in the context of a broad base of scientific knowledge.

We admire the spirit of modal empiricism as an intended alternative to modal rationalism. Modal empiricism is an active research programme, and it remains to be fully evaluated whether and in what ways its unique theoretical frameworks are preferable to traditional rationalist ones. When we motivate modal naturalism with scientific examples in Sections 8 and 9 and outline its comparative virtues in Section 10, we believe that modal naturalism will emerge as a satisfying alternative to both.

6 Counterfactual Accounts

6.1 Counterfactuals and Modal Epistemology

Counterfactual accounts of modal epistemology claim that the source of modal knowledge is the ability to reason counterfactually, imagine counterfactual scenarios, or assess counterfactual conditionals. The views account for modal knowledge in terms of our ordinary ability to infer or imagine what would happen were such-and-such to occur: for instance, that the lights would go out were I to flip the switch to the 'off' position. Proponents of this sort of view include Dohrn (2020), Hill (2006), Kroedel (2012, 2017), Lange (2005), and Williamson (2007). We will focus on Williamson's account, which has been widely influential.

Williamson considers his counterfactual modal epistemology neither rationalist nor empiricist, since it characterises modal knowledge neither as purely a priori nor as purely a posteriori. In his view, the distinction 'obscures . . . significant epistemic patterns' (2007, 169) – a point which we have echoed here. According to Williamson, while modal knowledge can be gained from the armchair, it nevertheless '[does] not fit the stereotype of the a priori, because the contribution of experience [is] far more than enabling' (2007, 169). The role of experience is more than enabling because of the centrality of counterfactual thinking to modal knowledge, together with the fact that counterfactual thought is 'deeply integrated into our empirical thought in general' (2007, 141). In Williamson's view, 'the ordinary cognitive capacity to handle counterfactual conditionals carries with it the cognitive capacity to handle metaphysical modality' (2007, 136). Thus the story of modal knowledge is really the story of counterfactual knowledge.

Williamson claims that this story is developmental and evolutionarily unmysterious. As one grows and learns, experience conditions us into 'patterns of expectation which are called on in [our] assessment of ordinary counterfactual conditionals' (2007, 167). We gradually accrue a background of empirical knowledge that informs everyday counterfactual thoughts, like 'If the bush had not been there, the rock would have ended in the lake' (2007, 142). Our counterfactual thinking often invokes the imagination, 'radically informed and disciplined' by the empirical background of beliefs and an accompanying folk physics (2007, 143). Imagination frequently plays a role, but not always, since 'imaginative simulation is neither always necessary nor always sufficient' for the evaluation of counterfactuals (2007, 152). In sum, according to Williamson's account, much modal knowledge is to be accounted for in terms of counterfactual knowledge.

One might wonder how far our counterfactual capacities get us in terms of generating modal knowledge. Arguably, our capacities for counterfactual reasoning, shaped as they are by the actual world and its features, prepare us to reason well about ordinary cases and worlds like our own. While those capacities equip us to reason through mundane counterfactual scenarios, it is less clear that they equip us to reason through strange and distant ones. For instance, a person may know that it is possible to leave her desk because it's a normal enough scenario – she has at her disposal an empirically informed and relevant background of belief about her own abilities and prior actions. But it is less clear what equips her to evaluate the possibility of zombies, swampmen, and other science fiction philosophical inventions.

In light of this, one might worry that counterfactual accounts don't sufficiently underwrite reliability for the typical activities of philosophers doing what we have called extensional modal metaphysics. Such accounts may well describe everyday modal reasoning yet do less well at capturing the more esoteric explorations of distant possible worlds that metaphysicians often pursue. Counterfactual imagination is an impressive human ability, but it works best in familiar domains – tracking the capacities of people, other animals, plants, rivers, clouds, and the like, and extrapolating these capacities to imagine things like gods, dragons, and aliens. We cannot be so well assured of the reliability of its deliverances when applied to things further from our evolutionary milieu.

This is not to say that counterfactual accounts are wrong, but simply that they do not vindicate modal metaphysical practice. From our point of view, this is not necessarily a negative feature of these views.[26] If modal knowledge is a function of a capacity for mundane counterfactual reasoning, then to whatever extent our more esoteric modal claims go beyond mundane counterfactual reasoning – or at any rate are too unlike mundane claims to be supported by it – they risk failing to count as modal knowledge. One might embrace this as a consequence of the view, rather than a problem for it, and adopt a revisionist attitude toward modal metaphysics according to which modal metaphysicians should avoid speculation about more esoteric and distant possible worlds. Alternatively, proponents

---

[26] Moreover, it is a feature shared by other frameworks, some of which explicitly set out to account for ordinary cases, for example, Roca-Royes' (2017).

of counterfactual accounts could seek independent explanations of putative knowledge of worlds very unlike our own.

From our perspective, the main limitation of Williamson's counterfactual account in particular is in its reliance on what he calls *constitutive facts* (Williamson 2007, 164, 170). These facts are held fixed in our counterfactual reasoning in a distinctive manner; Williamson mentions the classic case of gold having atomic number 79, often identified as an example of the necessary a posteriori. No further account is given of the nature of constitutive facts or of what licences their universal fixedness within counterfactual reasoning.

There are two main ways in which the reliance on constitutive facts might be used against Williamson's account. The first is to follow Yli-Vakkuri (2013) in arguing that the role of constitutive facts renders the counterfactual element of Williamson's account redundant: the objection is that we can replace counterfactual development of scenarios holding fixed constitutive facts with simple deductive reasoning using constitutive facts as premises. The second line of thought, which we prefer, focuses on the epistemology of the constitutive facts themselves (Roca-Royes 2011; Tahko 2012; Mallozzi 2020, 2021). If the counterfactual approach has nothing distinctive to say about how we know that *gold has atomic number 79* is a constitutive fact, then it is at best an incomplete modal epistemology.

6.2 Counterfactual Accounts and Modal Naturalism

For our purposes, the most pressing question is whether counterfactual accounts of modal epistemology are naturalistic in our sense. Given the central justificatory role of constitutive facts in Williamson's version, and given how relatively little he says about our knowledge of them, his account leaves open some of the key questions of this Element. The counterfactual approach can be filled out in both naturalistic and non-naturalistic ways. For example, if constitutive facts were identified in significant part via a priori intuition or similar routes, then the overall modal epistemology would have rationalist foundations. By contrast, if we fill out the account by identifying a primary role for scientific investigation in producing our knowledge of constitutive facts, then the view assigns a key justificatory role to scientific knowledge underpinning modal knowledge more broadly and tends instead in the modal naturalist direction.

It is important to distinguish the plausible thesis that science can bear evidentially on the constitutive facts themselves – that we can discover scientifically, for example, that gold has atomic number 79 – from the much more controversial thesis that science can bear evidentially on which facts are constitutive facts. To be fully naturalistic, Williamson's account would need to implicate science both in the first-order knowledge of constitutive facts and the higher-order knowledge of which facts are constitutive – since the latter is crucial for determining what should be held fixed throughout counterfactual reasoning. Since Williamson does not mandate the latter role for science in enabling modal knowledge, his modal epistemology is not expressly naturalistic.

In summary, while counterfactual accounts have their own distinctive focus, they can complement modal naturalism so long as they do not assign evidential weight to unchecked a priori capacities in the problematic ways we have discussed throughout the Element. To count as naturalistic, counterfactual accounts need to tie knowledge of the modal facts directly to science. For instance, a naturalistic counterfactual modal epistemology might identify the counterfactual inferences embedded in science as an especially important or privileged route to modal knowledge, or might reconstruct central scientific discoveries of modal facts in counterfactual terms.

6.3 Summary

In this section, we have discussed counterfactual accounts of the epistemology of modal facts, focusing on Williamson's influential account. We identified an epistemic challenge to his view concerning the identification of constitutive facts. We argued that counterfactual-based views are (as so far stated) neutral on the question of modal naturalism, and that they can be filled out in more or less naturalistic ways. Counterfactual accounts like Williamson's that assign a central role to constitutive facts, if they can answer the challenge concerning the redundancy of the counterfactual development part of their modal epistemology, and if they can provide a plausible scientific route to the identification and justification of constitutive facts, are potentially congenial to the modal naturalist.

7 Relatives of Modal Naturalism

We have now characterised the modal naturalist programme and situated it within the broader theoretical landscape of standard modal epistemological frameworks. Our positive arguments for modal naturalism will follow in subsequent sections – based on discussion of some specific cases in Sections 8 and 9 and on more general considerations in Section 10. Before turning to those arguments, our position can be further explicated by considering more closely how modal naturalism relates to non-rationalist views in the same general vicinity. While we cannot provide a full assessment of each of these views, we hope to say enough to make clear how they relate to our own proposal.

7.1 Modal Empiricism

We gave reasons in Section 5 to think that modal naturalism and modal empiricism are distinct kinds of view. Still, one might wonder precisely how these views relate to one another, and in particular whether modal empiricism and modal naturalism approach each other closely enough for one to be a species of the other.

On our conception of modal naturalism, we do not see it as a species of modal empiricism but rather as standing outside the rationalist/empiricist dichotomy as a sui generis theoretical alternative. In our view, the a priori/a posteriori distinction is not the neatest, most helpful, or most relevant joint to carve at here. Modal naturalism is not in the final analysis about how modal knowledge is classified with respect to the a priori or the a posteriori. Rather, like the counterfactual accounts discussed in the last section, modal naturalism aims to be a distinct theoretical alternative that fits neatly into neither pre-established camp – modal rationalism or modal empiricism. Science is the epistemically relevant category, it integrates both a priori and a posteriori elements, and its successes are not solely attributable to the one or the other.

Though modal naturalism is not a species of modal empiricism, might the reverse be true? That is, could some of the stronger forms of modal empiricism, such as Roca-Royes' (2017) and Fischer's (2016, 2017) accounts, be considered forms of modal naturalism? Consider Roca-Royes' similarity-based account, according to which we extrapolate knowledge of objects' unrealised possibilities from knowledge of the realised possibilities of similar objects. While science may have some role to play in obtaining the initial knowledge, the role of science is not built into the view in quite the way the naturalist would want. Science and scientific ways of knowing may inform us about realised possibilities and equip us with categorical knowledge, but to be naturalistic, the proponent of the similarity-based view would need to tie modal knowledge more directly to these forms of support. Moreover, as we will show in subsequent sections, the modal naturalist believes that science does a good deal more for us vis-à-vis modal knowledge than acquainting us with realised possibilities or filling in categorical knowledge. For these reasons, we do not see Roca-Royes' similarity-based account as a form of modal naturalism, though more explicitly naturalistic extensions or variants of the view are possible (see, for instance, Wirling 2022).

Turning now to Fischer's theory-based account: as we remarked in Section 5, a theory-based account that indexes (at least some forms of) modal knowledge to our best theories needs to say which sorts of theories count as best and why. Fischer acknowledges that his account needs to be paired with 'a story about how we can justifiably believe (some) theories' (2017, 17), but leaves this story open to be filled in. He explains that the theory-based approach 'builds the epistemology on the back of your epistemology for theories. If you are a scientific realist – or a naturalistically minded metaphysician – then you need to explain how we can justifiably believe some of our best theories' (2017, 17–18). We take this as a signal that the theory-based framework is compatible in the abstract with modal naturalism, without explicitly committing to it. Nevertheless, Fischer seems to closely associate our best theories with physical theories (2017, 33) and with scientific theorising (2017, 76 and 127). He also gives the following example, which shows how the theory-based account can recognise a role for science: 'If our best biology implies that you can make a dinosaur by inserting certain genes into a chicken egg, then the evidence for that biology is evidence that nothing precludes making such a creature' (2017, 14). This sort of example is congenial to modal naturalism.

However, the centrality of scientific evidence needs to be made explicit for a theory-based account to count as a form of modal naturalism. To the modal naturalist, it is not enough to say there *can* be a role for science in generating modal knowledge; rather, modal naturalism enshrines science as the centrepiece of its distinctive modal epistemology. So, while Fischer's theory-based account approaches modal naturalism more closely than other forms of modal empiricism, the naturalist would want such an account to appropriately restrict the range of theories that are recognised as sources of modal knowledge to reflect science's distinguished status and special bearing on modal claims. As with the similarity-based account, the theory-based account is not quite naturalistic as canonically stated, but naturalistic variants could be articulated.

7.2 Modal Psychology

Setting modal empiricism aside, there are other approaches to modal epistemology and metaphysics that have been characterised as 'naturalistic'. Nolan (2017) proposes a naturalistic modal epistemology, which uses scientific techniques to investigate various dimensions of our practices of modal judgement. In particular, he suggests that naturalistic modal epistemology might involve studying the psychology of modal reasoning among children and adults, the perception of affordances, the linguistics of natural language modals, and the social function of modal judgement (2017, 19–22). Nolan also suggests that a naturalistic modal epistemology attends to the role of modality in science itself, as well as to the processes by which science generates its modal content. For instance, he claims that modality can receive naturalistic vindication if it is shown to be indispensable to science (2017, 22); moreover, in studying how science gets and modifies its modal content, he claims we can identify methods that reliably generate modal knowledge (2017, 23–24).

While the naturalistic project Nolan recommends is valuable, the project we envisage here differs in spirit and in letter.

First, the spirit of our project is decidedly less permissive than Nolan's. He claims that 'one can be a naturalist without condemning a lot of work that is already being done on modality' (Nolan 2017, 13), and that 'methodological naturalism has a place for relying on intuitions, for something like old-fashioned conceptual analysis, and bringing our modal opinions into equilibrium with our other philosophical commitments' (Nolan 2017, 19). By contrast, our modal naturalism has a more critical and revisionary spirit. We reject modal rationalism and aim to provide an attractive alternative to it which reins in what we see as an untenable reliance on purely a priori methods.

Second, the substance of our naturalistic prescriptions differs from Nolan's. While Nolan recommends that the naturalist scientifically study various dimensions of modal judgement, as well as the aetiology of science's modal content, we recommend that the naturalist also attend directly to the modal content of science in assessing the extensional modal metaphysical facts. We are not in the first instance interested in how science can illuminate our reasoning about the modal facts but rather in how it can illuminate the modal facts themselves. Rather than using science to investigate modal knowledge, then, we wish to carve out a central role for science in the justification of modal claims. By analogy to the field of moral psychology, Nolan's project strikes us as being more directly akin to modal psychology than it is to modal epistemology.

7.3 'Moderately Naturalistic' Metaphysics

The title of Morganti and Tahko (2017) promises a 'moderately naturalistic' metaphysics, and the paper is largely concerned with modal epistemology; one might expect this modal epistemology to be at least moderately naturalistic. However, its approach to modal epistemology has too much of a residual rationalist character to qualify as modal naturalism, as we have defined the view. Morganti and Tahko defend a view of metaphysics inspired by E.J. Lowe, according to which metaphysics is 'primarily concerned with a priori arguments for the *possibility* of certain ontological categories and hypotheses' (Morganti and Tahko 2017, 2566). In their view, metaphysics informs the interpretation of science, and science is, in turn, 'at least an indirect 'testing ground' for metaphysical hypotheses' (2017, 2561). That is, metaphysics identifies a range of possibilities by identifying 'coherent alternatives' (2017, 2576), some of which ultimately crop up in physical theories and are thereby shown to be 'workable, worth consideration and also capable of accounting for the available empirical data' (2017, 2577). For instance, the possibility of metaphysical infinitism 'whereby there simply is no ultimate layer of reality' (2017, 2566) crops up in Hans Dehmelt's physical theory, 'whereby an infinite series of layers of three particles each leads towards Dirac point particles in the limit' (2017, 2577).

In Morganti and Tahko's view, the possibilities identified by the metaphysician are indirectly testable in the sense that they frame certain physical models which are themselves testable. From what we can tell, though, the contribution of science in this view is to bear out wholly a priori modal conjectures. Tahko and Morganti describe this contribution as a 'validation' of the possibilities discovered a priori; yet what the modal naturalist wants is not post hoc validation but rather ex ante justification for taking something to be possible. If their idea of scientific validation is not just a matter of making us feel better about our a priori speculations, Morganti and Tahko don't explain what more it amounts to. For these reasons, we consider their 'moderately naturalistic' approach to be insufficiently naturalistic.

We would place the view of Mallozzi (2020, 2021) in a similar category. Mallozzi's view centres around modal metaphysical knowledge of essences, which she conceives of as causal and explanatory properties that unify natural kinds and that are 'identified by the results of the natural sciences' (Mallozzi 2021, S1952). Her version of scientific essentialism is clearly in the vicinity of modal naturalism, given her emphasis on science as our best route to knowledge of individual essences, and her claim that the metaphysics and epistemology of metaphysical modality proceed 'hand in hand with scientific investigation' (2021, S1954). However, Mallozzi makes a sharp division between the scientific and a priori components of modal epistemology, arguing that a priori bridge principles are required to draw any modal conclusions from knowledge of essence; she also allows that large parts of our modal knowledge might be entirely a priori, potentially requiring an independent epistemological treatment in terms of 'conceptual entailment from real definitions' (Mallozzi 2021, S1952). This willingness to assign more than an enabling role to independent a priori reasoning suggests that, as with Morganti and Tahko's view, Mallozzi's view should not ultimately be counted as a version of modal naturalism.

7.4 Projectivist Views

We turn next to a very different class of views of modality and its associated epistemology that might also be labelled 'naturalism': proposals such as those of Hirvonen et al. (2021), Ismael (2017), and Price (2004), which aim to account for practices of modal commitment and discourse in science in a way that satisfies empiricists, pragmatists, and other theorists who regard metaphysics with suspicion. Such views are regarded as naturalistic because they decline to pursue empirically intractable and metaphysically lofty questions about the metaphysics of modality and instead attend to the empirically tractable domains of cognition and language use.

These views fall under a broader category that we will label 'projectivism', since they tend to agree that our modal theorising is ultimately a matter of a projection of some aspect of our own cognitive lives. Fellow members of this broader category include Blackburn (1993) and Thomasson (2020). While projectivist views are of independent interest, we think they lack direct bearing on the kind of modal naturalism we have in mind. The naturalism involved in a projectivist outlook is a naturalism at the metaphilosophical level, which places empirically tractable practices at the centre of inquiry, rather than a naturalism at the epistemological level, which prescribes a science-centred epistemology for modality conceived as a domain of mind-independent facts.

While we appreciate the spirit of these views and their contribution to our understanding of the modal content of science, we see modal naturalism as pursuing different ends. Rather than accounting for modal dimensions of scientific practice in a metaphysically minimal way, the modal naturalist regards science as an important source of modal metaphysical knowledge. Nevertheless, projectivism and modal naturalism in our sense are not incompatible; one could simultaneously hold that while modality itself is of our own making, nonetheless we have made modality in such a way that modal naturalism is the correct account of its first-order epistemology. However, there is at least some tension here: some central motivations for modal naturalism, concerning our epistemic access to modal facts and their rational relevance to us, seem to be undercut by a projectivist account of modal reality that renders the access question and the relevance question misconceived (Thomasson 2020). Our modal naturalist assumes a straightforwardly realist treatment of modal facts and takes seriously questions about the knowability and relevance of these facts.

7.5 Modal Science

While none of the views we have discussed so far have been clearly identifiable as forms of modal naturalism, Williamson's 'Modal Science' (2016) more closely approaches the kind of modal naturalism that we propose. In that paper, Williamson argues that objective modal knowledge is an integrated component of scientific knowledge. Scientific laws support subjunctive conditionals, and when they do so successfully over time, we have abductive grounds for thinking they are nomically necessary. Moreover, Williamson argues, the quantification of objective probabilities we find in, for instance, the interpretation of statistics, the formulation of quantum mechanics, and the derivation of standard thermodynamic principles from classical statistical mechanics, presupposes a form of objective modality. Finally, dynamical systems theory employs state spaces – abstract spaces of objective possibility – the topological features of which are integral to the theory's explanatory power.

To the extent that scientists reason about possible states of physical systems, '[n]atural science studies the structure of spaces of objective possibilities just as much as metaphysics does' (2016, 479). So natural science investigates objective modality. Williamson concludes that we should not 'treat the metaphysics and epistemology of metaphysical modality in isolation from the metaphysics and epistemology of the natural sciences' (2016, 453). On all these points, Williamson and the modal naturalist are kindred spirits. Our case for modal naturalism in Section 10 will draw on similar considerations, in particular on the ubiquity of modalised models in science and on the distinctive explanatory role of state spaces (Section 10.1).

7.6 Summary

This section has elucidated the relationships between modal naturalism and various seemingly related non-rationalisms. We claimed that modal naturalism is not a species of modal empiricism, because it declines to situate itself relative to the a priori/a posteriori distinction. Neither similarity-based nor theory-based modal empiricisms are forms of modal naturalism as canonically stated, but we have acknowledged the potential for more explicitly naturalistic variants of these views. The project of modal naturalism and that of what we describe as modal psychology are importantly distinct. 'Moderately naturalistic metaphysics' does not furnish a suitably naturalistic modal epistemology. While views that regard modal theorising as a projection of features of our cognitive lives might be regarded as naturalistic given the empirically tractable nature of their claims, they do not share the modal naturalist's commitment to mind-independent modal facts. Finally, to the extent that Williamson's 'Modal Science' acknowledges the distinctive contribution of science to modal knowledge, it counts as a form of modal naturalism.

Now that we have described modal naturalism and contextualised it amongst related accounts, it is time to present some positive arguments for the view. In the next two sections, we outline and explore a number of candidate examples of scientific discoveries of modal facts, before turning to more general arguments for the view in Section 10.

8 Scientific Discoveries of Possibilities

In this section, we look at a variety of candidate examples of scientific discoveries of previously unknown possibilities. In Section 9, we turn to the flipside: cases which may be described as the scientific discovery of previously unknown impossibilities. The cases in these two sections together comprise our primary line of argument for modal naturalism, since we take modal naturalism to give a more plausible account of these cases than alternative modal epistemologies.

We start with a lead example – curved spacetime – and then extend a similar treatment to other phenomena from fundamental physics. In each case, our view of the physical world has changed so radically that the explanatory structures currently postulated by physicists would have historically been presumed impossible. These examples from physics are, we think, the most clear-cut. We then move to some more contentious examples from biology and psychology; at least on some reasonable interpretations, these cases may also be considered examples of scientific discovery of previously unknown possibilities.

Along the way we will encounter many examples of science apparently upending previously held modal beliefs. This might suggest a pessimistic inference: even if we pay close attention to contemporary science in forming our modal beliefs, then we are still liable to end up with false modal beliefs. Given our broadly scientific realist assumptions, we set this problem aside here. However, if you are inclined to worry that the pessimistic meta-induction shows that we can't expect to get scientifically-based modal knowledge, then we suggest a lowering of epistemic ambitions. You might not be able to get modal *knowledge* from a modal naturalist approach, but at least you'll get the *best-justified* modal beliefs available at any given time. We think that is still better than what you'd get from taking a modal rationalist approach.

By way of clarification: the cases in these sections do not need to be understood from a necessitarian perspective in order to provide support for modal naturalism. While these cases are certainly compatible with the higher grades of modal naturalism (grade 2 and above) from Section 3.4, the cases in this section require only commitment to the more moderate grade 1 modal naturalism.

8.1 Cases from Revolutions in Physics

Physics in the late nineteenth century seemed – at least to some – to be nearing completion. The physical world, as captured by deterministic classical field theories, was a neat and orderly place. Radical foundational upheaval seemed unlikely. But nature took physicists, and the rest of us, by surprise; the successive conceptual revolutions of relativistic mechanics and quantum theory leave us now contemplating a much stranger physical world.

Some of the most exotic entities envisaged by modern physics – black holes, quarks, quantum computers – present enduring challenges to understanding and are often explained by appeal to imperfect metaphors, which at least have the virtue of familiarity. The difficulty, if not impossibility, of fully visualising a four-dimensional space obliges us to introduce theories, like general relativity, using curved surface diagrams that suppress at least one spatial dimension. Characteristically, cases where we still cannot successfully visualise some aspect of the current scientific worldview tend to correspond to things that would have been reckoned straightforwardly impossible by the standards of many previous systematic pictures of the world.

Perhaps the clearest example of a scientific discovery of possibility – and one that is much celebrated in the history of philosophy of science – is the discovery of the possibility of curved spacetime geometry around the turn of the twentieth century. (This discovery subsumes the remarkable unification of space and time into spacetime memorably expressed by Minkowski (1952).) In the curved spacetime case, there was not much of a historical gap between recognition of the mathematical coherence of curved spaces by mathematicians including Riemann and acknowledgement of the actuality of curved spacetime as part of general relativity. The conceptual transformation was dramatic – within one or two generations, curved spacetime went from being a bizarre mathematical curiosity of dubious coherence to being part of physicists' standard worldview.

There is clearly no allowance for even the metaphysical possibility of curved spacetime – or even of spacetime as opposed to space and time – in the worldview of classical physics as it was predominantly understood. Under the influence of first Newton and then Kant, Euclidean space was presented as an unchanging and unchangeable background for dynamics to play out in. Kant in particular was explicit: possible experience requires constant mutual action at a distance, and hence requires the notion of absolute simultaneity which Newtonian physics supports but relativistic physics does not. Einstein saw his own work as decisively refuting Kant here (Einstein 1918, letter to Max Born). Curved spacetime, then, gives us our central motivating case of a scientific discovery of possibility. On our reading, there was a shift in scientific opinion sometime between 1850 and 1950 from a consensus view that curved spacetime is impossible to a consensus view that it is possible.

In retrospect, it is possible to reinterpret earlier theories as involving curved space and/or spacetime. Newton-Cartan theory (see e.g. Malament 1986; Knox 2011) formulates Newtonian mechanics without a gravitational force using the mathematical tools of curved spacetime. Motions that in the ordinary formulation of Newtonian gravitation are explained by the action of a gravitational force are reinterpreted in Newton-Cartan theory as geodesic ('natural') motions of bodies moving freely in a curved background space. There are interesting philosophical questions to ask about whether these formulations are distinct theories, and about whether we could in principle tell which one is correct. If we do regard Newton-Cartan theory as describing a possibility distinct from that of ordinary Newtonian gravity, then it follows that there were further objective possibilities inherent in classical physics which were nonetheless judged impossible by the prevailing metaphysical opinions of the era. By contrast, from a more functionalist point of view (Knox 2011), there is in fact no distinct possibility here, since spacetime structure should not be automatically determined by the metric.

Theoretical reformulations cut both ways. Teleparallel gravity is a reformulation of general relativity which casts it in terms of a complex gravitational force law operative against a flat background spacetime.[27] It is potentially open to traditionalists to point to the availability of these theories in order to maintain that (after all) there is no actuality – and hence potentially no objective possibility – of curved spacetime after all. This seems to be the position taken by, for example, Andrade and Pereira (1997); but it is a significant minority view within spacetime physics, and we set it aside here. The overwhelming majority view amongst contemporary physicists is that spacetime can be curved, and that we know this fact as a result of doing physics.

Curved spacetime is in fact the common factor of a whole family of examples of scientific discovery of possibility that can be drawn from modern gravitational physics. In general relativity, the presence of nearby massive objects leads to time dilation: clocks tick slower when close to the surface of the earth than when at a distance. In other words, it is possible for mass to slow down time. This effect can readily be demonstrated with atomic clocks in aeroplanes, and it needs to be compensated for in order to maintain time synchronisation of GPS satellites. Proximity to a massive object also leads to precession in the rotation of orbiting bodies: the celebrated calculation of the precession of the perihelion of Mercury by Einstein in 1915 was an important early piece of evidence supporting general relativity. Frame-dragging is a related dynamical effect, also mediated by curved spacetime, in which rotating objects precess differently when the object they are orbiting is rotating than when it is not rotating. All these effects are wholly absent in classical mechanics. In fact, they would typically have been regarded as simply impossible by those immersed in the worldview of classical mechanics. Black holes, being locations of radically curved spacetime, incorporate the effects just described, but they have

---

[27] Again, from a functionalist point of view (Knox 2011), teleparallel gravity does not in fact involve a spacetime ontology distinct from that of general relativity.

peculiarities of their own. Even without getting into quantum effects such as Hawking radiation, black holes have event horizons – surfaces from inside which nothing, including light, can escape (without quantum tunnelling) leading to the holes' blackness. The discovery of the possibility of black holes was a scientific sensation.

A second and even more diverse family of examples of scientific discovery of possibility can be drawn from quantum theory. As always with quantum theory, the exact lessons to be drawn will depend on which theoretical interpretation we prefer, but there are some quantum phenomena which seem to require recognition of novel possibilities on many or all plausible interpretations. A first category of examples here comes from quantum tunnelling, such as that which goes on in radioactive alpha decay. In quantum theory (but not in classical physics) a particle can spontaneously cross an energy barrier to escape from a potential well even when the energy required classically to cross the barrier exceeds that present in the system. A related phenomenon is the creation and rapid annihilation of virtual particle-antiparticle pairs. On plausible interpretations of quantum field theory, this effect is not the creation of something ex nihilo but a transition between different states of the field. The upshot is that in quantum field theory, even 'empty' spacetime is full of activity: in this (very constrained) sense, we have discovered something can come from nothing.

Beyond tunnelling phenomena, Bell correlations constitute a further striking feature of quantum theory – a feature which again is wholly absent from classical mechanics. In cases where entangled particle systems are separated in space, so that measurements on the two are outside each others' regions of causal influence, the measurement outcomes nevertheless can remain correlated in a way that provably lacks a local causal explanation. The experimental verification of these predictions occasioned the award of the physics Nobel Prize for 2022. We might, of course, question whether this quantum action at a distance is a genuine instance of modal discovery; didn't Newtonian gravitation already feature action at a distance? Saying much more on this point would require delving into the details of the different interpretations of quantum theory, but in general we can say that any approach which assigns entangled systems non-separable physical states (including many-worlds quantum mechanics, the Ghirardi-Rimini-Weber dynamical-collapse theory, and some versions of Bohmian mechanics) will involve a significant departure from what was considered a necessary truth about physical systems: that the state of a compound system supervenes on their individual states, plus their spatiotemporal relations. For further discussion, see Teller (1986) and Schaffer and Ismael (2020).

Finally, most interpretations of quantum theory involve indeterminism of some kind. In collapse theories, the dynamics are indeterministic; in many-worlds approaches, there is effective indeterminism from the in-world perspective; and even in hidden-variables approaches like Bohmian mechanics, it might still be most natural to understand probabilities through an initial indeterministic chance event (Demarest 2016). Once again, this conflicts with what Kant (1781/1998) argued in the Analogies of Experience to be a necessary precondition of any possible experience; more generally, determinism was a conceptual pillar of classical physics and not seriously questioned as a framing assumption for modern physics until the rise of quantum theory. However, it turns out that some of our best interpretations of quantum theory make it possible for events to occur without their being determined to occur.

All the aforementioned examples, if they succeed, were discovered to be possible in virtue of being discovered to be actual. But we can also gain indirect evidence for the possibility of certain non-actual scenarios. A model of some physical theory corresponding to the actual world is part of a larger set of models, and attending to those models can give us evidence for the possibilities to which they correspond.

For a first example of this, it has been argued that string theory gives us evidence for the possibility of different dimensionalities of effective space-time, corresponding to different minima of the string theory 'landscape' (see Susskind 2006 for an accessible introduction to the string landscape). In the string landscape scenario, it is a quantum-mechanically contingent matter which dimensionality of effective spacetime emerges from the fundamental higher-dimensional background spacetime; thus insofar as we can get empirical evidence for the string landscape hypothesis, we can get empirical evidence for the possibility of effective spacetimes of dimensionality larger than our actual 3+1.

A less conjectural example comes from potential super-heavy chemical elements. No elements with atomic number above 118 have ever been synthesised, and it is quite plausible that, for example, unsepttrium (with atomic number 173) will never exist in our visible universe. Nonetheless, theoretical chemists can model at least some of its properties such as energy eigenvalues to explore how unsepttrium would behave if it were to exist (Fricke and Soff 1977): it is predicted to behave like a highly reactive alkali metal, for the few microseconds its isotopes could exist before decaying. In these examples, it seems that theoretical physics and theoretical chemistry can result in genuine modal discovery that is not simply a logical consequence of a discovery of the actual.

8.2 Cases from Higher-Level Sciences

Moving beyond physics, historical approaches to biology included many constraints that modern biology violates; our suggestion is that a failure to respect these constraints would have been regarded as impossible by the standards of previous approaches. For example, Aristotelian species are generally understood to have been fixed and immutable over time; the prospect of a human evolving from an ape would have been considered not only absurd but impossible – contrary to the very nature of things – from an Aristotelian perspective. Even a mixture of characteristics across families, as occurs in (for example) the duck-billed platypus, might contravene assumed necessities concerning the distinctive characteristics of creatures. Indeed, when the first individuals were returned from Australia to Europe, naturalists were initially inclined to dismiss them as obvious fakes – for how could any natural thing possibly combine features characteristic of birds (bill and egg-laying) with features characteristic of mammals (fur and lactation), without contravening the underlying essences of the species falling under these classes? Relatedly, we take the discovery of evolution to have been at least partly constituted by the modal discovery that individual species can change and diversify over time.

A final type of example comes from cognitive science: the alleged possibility of reliably predicting human action prior to the agent's consciousness of their own decisions. On a face-value reading, the experiments performed by Libet (Libet et al. 1983) show that there are reliably measurable predictive markers available in the electrical activity of a person's brain that make it very probable that the person is about to act in a certain way – for example, to press a button – before the time at which the person reports a conscious awareness of having made a final decision. These experiments are extraordinarily controversial (see Mele 2008 for discussion), and we don't want to take any stand on what they do or don't show about free will. But, we suggest, historically their experimental results would have often been regarded as impossible (or at least: their reliable replication would have been regarded as impossible) in the context of libertarian approaches to human freedom.

As with theoretical physics and chemistry, there is room for modal discovery in higher-level sciences that goes via theoretical routes. Ecology and zoology might in principle provide evidence for the possibility of certain biological species via theoretical considerations concerning evolutionary niches – even if, as a matter of actual fact, those biological species never evolved and never will. Likewise theoretical economics might help us identify a novel possible economic equilibrium state, even if no actual economy ever has or ever will operate within the circumstances which lead to that particular equilibrium. Here, the literature on how-possibly explanations in higher-level science is a further source of potential examples. For example, Verreault-Julien (2019) discusses a number of cases in which attention to theoretical models helps identify a possible causal pathway by which a given phenomenon may arise, including the explanation of demographic segregation in terms of individual choices offered by Schelling (1971). In some cases at least, these pathways will correspond to possible but non-actual causal histories; in these cases, we have further examples of scientific discovery of non-actual possibilities.

8.3 Summary

In this section we have drawn attention to a number of examples from the history of science and argued that they constitute cases of genuine modal discovery in virtue of revealing new objective possibilities. These cases range from the universal and fundamental – the shape of space, the constitution of matter, the nature of probability – to principles which structure inquiry in the special sciences, including biology and cognitive science. Some of these cases were simply never envisaged by prior philosophical thought; but others were actively rejected, as when Kant identified determinism and absolute simultaneity as preconditions for any possible experience. Although individual cases can of course be disputed, our intention with these cases is to draw attention to the variety of the ways in which science might reveal new possibilities and hence to contribute to a broad abductive case for modal naturalism.

9 Scientific Discoveries of Impossibilities

Possibility and necessity are generally regarded as duals:[28] when one finds out that P is possible, one finds out that it is not the case that not-P is necessary. So all of the discoveries of possibilities highlighted in the previous section are ipso facto discoveries that certain necessities do not hold. For example, the empirical evidence in favour of general relativity, which has convinced most observers that it is possible that spacetime be curved, counts equally as evidence that it is not necessary that spacetime be flat. In addition, assuming S5 modal logic, any discoveries of possibilities are ipso facto discoveries of necessities, since possibility claims are themselves necessary.

Are there interesting cases of scientific discovery of necessities that are not directly parasitic on some discovery of possibility in the ways just highlighted? We think that there are, and in this section we discuss some of the most interesting potential examples. We should note at the outset that to take seriously the cases

---

[28] Though see Cowling (2011) and Goswick (2015) for reasons to doubt this.

discussed in this section requires signing up to one of the higher grades from Section 3. Grade 2 is required at minimum if these examples are to motivate modal naturalism.

Of course, those who reject grade 2 or higher modal naturalism may give their own accounts of these cases. Typically they will say – for example – that the impossibility of a perpetual motion machine of the second kind is not absolute: all that is impossible is the co-instantiation of a perpetual motion machine of the second kind and the actual laws of nature. At grades 0 and 1, the cases we will discuss must be understood as showing us something about what is and is not compatible with the actual laws of nature, and no support for modal naturalism accrues. We do not aim to refute this deflationary reading of these cases. Our claims are twofold – firstly, that at higher grades of modal naturalism these cases amount to scientific discovery of limits to objective possibility, and secondly that this treatment fits naturally with the way these discoveries are characterised by scientists and with the significance that they accord them. The section thereby forms part of our broader abductive case for modal naturalism.

9.1 Mechanical Impossibilities

Our first candidate case of a substantive discovery of necessity comes from thermodynamics. There are limits on the maximum efficiency of a heat engine: as Carnot discovered, this maximum efficiency is equal to the ratio of the absolute temperatures of the heat reservoirs involved. It is necessary that every working heat engine has an efficiency no higher than this ratio; perpetual motion machines ('of the second kind'), which extract work from heat, are therefore impossible. Although it is in principle possible (in so-called 'deviant' microstates) for heat to decrease and work to increase, the probability of this is vanishingly small, and there is no possibility of causing or controlling its occurrence. So the point stands: perpetual motion machines of the second kind are impossible to build. This was a surprising discovery, and deeply disappointing to some; to this day, patent offices continue to receive applications for patents for heat-to-work machines.

The limitation which Carnot discovered on thermodynamic behaviour may be understood using statistical mechanics and hence ultimately may be explained in terms of the underlying mechanics of the system. But the reducibility of thermodynamics to statistical mechanics does not prevent thermodynamics encoding a substantive modal discovery: given the kind of systems heat engines are and the kind of matter that we are made of, there is simply no metaphysically possible way to build a perpetual motion machine of the second kind. From the necessitarian perspective which we are adopting in this section, the impossibility here is not merely physical, since it flows from the actual nature of matter; anything which could be induced into perpetual motion would have to have a different constitution from our own universe's matter. The argument here parallels Bird's (2001) argument that salt necessarily dissolves in water. Anything with sufficiently different chemistry not to dissolve in water would have such a different constitution that it could not qualify as being salt.

Even a theory as familiar as classical mechanics seems to support a number of apparent necessities – the conservation of energy, of momentum, and of angular momentum, for example. Rather than being mere physical necessities, these conservation laws have intimate connections to the symmetries of the underlying physical description. Noether discovered that conservation principles may be derived from symmetries of the dynamical laws under certain general assumptions about the nature of mechanics. Noether's theorem, we suggest, accounts for the impossibility of energy non-conservation in classical mechanics in terms of a deep fact about the laws: that they are time-translation invariant, so that the laws do not 'care' what time it is. Any theory in which energy is not conserved would have to be time-translation non-invariant: physics would have to 'know what time it is' in order to determine how a system would evolve. And any theory in which angular momentum was not conserved would likewise have to feature a privileged direction in space. Insofar as the underlying metaphysics of the world is not rich enough to support facts about privileged times or privileged directions, there is no metaphysical possibility in which a world like ours, correctly described by a theory like classical mechanics, could fail to display energy conservation or angular momentum conservation.

Even if one doesn't regard time-translation invariance as a basic form of objective necessity (perhaps there are metaphysically possible laws which do care what time it is, even if they could not apply to our own universe), what is interesting about Noether's theorem is that it shows that conservation of energy at least has a higher degree of necessity than we previously supposed, in that it applies under all counterfactual scenarios in which time-translation invariance and the general (Lagrangian) form of the mechanics are maintained. Lange (2009) offers a detailed framework for reasoning about a hierarchy of degrees of necessity of this kind. On Lange's view, physics may provide us with evidence which bears on the degree of necessity of some given physical principle; this, we take it, is enough to vindicate at least a weak form of modal naturalism.

9.2 Quantum Impossibilities

Moving from classical to quantum physics furnishes new classes of examples of scientific discovery of necessity. In experimental setups to demonstrate the photoelectric effect, when a metal is illuminated with light which is below a minimum frequency, then no electrons can be ejected; the incoming photons are simply too low-energy to trigger the needed energy-level transition in the metal atoms. This latter impossibility could not be understood in terms of the wave theory of light, in which the intensity of an incoming wave could in principle be progressively increased to increase without limit the energy transferred to the incident surface, no matter the frequency.

More generally, there are plenty of classically allowable states that are simply not quantum-mechanically possible – excited states of atoms which have energies intermediate between lines in their actual atomic spectra, for example. A particularly consequential application of discovered quantum impossibility comes from quantum cryptography: it is not possible to read a message that has been quantum-mechanically encrypted while leaving its quantum state unchanged and hence without potentially revealing that one has been eavesdropping.

9.3 Spatiotemporal Impossibilities

Relativity theory offers us other classes of examples of discovered impossibility. One case is particularly clear and of great importance in the foundations of physics: information-bearing signals cannot be transmitted between spacelike separated observers. This holds true even in approaches to quantum theory which invoke non-local action at spacelike separation. On some approaches to combining quantum theory and relativity, this impossibility extends to any causal influence between the spacelike-separated observers; on other approaches, the impossibility only applies to causal influences being used to send signals. But in either case, the impossibility of signalling across spacelike separation appears to be a central component of what we have discovered scientifically about the nature of relativistic spacetime.

The laws discussed in this section up to this point, while not fundamental, have all been general, in that they apply across the known universe. But there are also necessities concerning spatiotemporal scale that can be discovered, which derive from laws that apply more locally – on planet Earth, for example. Here, given the prevailing gravitational and atmospheric conditions, there are hard limits on maximum and minimum body size and on body shapes.[29] We don't have elephant-sized ants or skyscraper-sized terrestrial animals – in fact, it's impossible for them to evolve (or even to survive for any length of time if somehow brought into being by a statistical-mechanical anomaly, quantum

---

[29] These allometric scaling constraints were mentioned by Galileo (1632/2023) and popularised by Haldane (1926).

fluke, or malevolent sorcerer). This impossibility is explained by the square-cube law, a simple law of geometry according to which when a square cube grows in size, its surface area increases by a power of 2, while its volume increases by a volume power of 3. If the size of an animal were to increase while keeping the same shape and proportions, various aspects of its physiology would cease to function. The respiratory and circulatory system of a giant insect would supply inadequate oxygen to the body; the bones of a real-life Godzilla wouldn't be strong enough to bear its weight.

9.4 Mathematical Impossibilities

We have focused throughout on discoveries in the natural sciences, but, of course, there have been substantive discoveries of impossibilities made throughout history by mathematicians, often mathematicians whose work was hard to fully disentangle from physics. For example, the problem of squaring the circle went from being considered too difficult for the human mind to resolve to being proved impossible in 1882. The challenge of finding a map that needs five colours to be coloured in without adjacent regions sharing a colour can be understood by a small child but was only proved impossible in 1976. In algebraic topology, the Borsak-Ulum theorem entails the initially extremely surprising result that, necessarily, there is at least one pair of antipodal (opposite) points on the Earth's surface with the same atmospheric pressure, another pair of antipodal points with the same air temperature, and so on for all continuously valued variables. These cases are all more-or-less surprising mathematical results, which, when applied to the natural world, generate cases of more-or-less surprising necessities. When we claim that science is our route to substantive modal discovery, we mean to include mathematics – or, at the very least, those portions of mathematics that are applicable to concrete phenomena.

9.5 Metaphysical Impossibilities

There is an additional class of cases of putative modal discovery, already discussed in Section 4: those which flow from discoveries concerning identity. This kind of discovery happens for example when science acquaints us with essential properties of chemical kinds (the well-worn identity water = H_2O) and numerical identities (Hesperus is Phosphorus). In discovering that water = H_2O, we thereby discover that it is not XYZ; and (assuming we know the necessity of identity, and draw the relevant inferences), we thereby discover that it is impossible for water to be XYZ. In discovering that Hesperus is Phosphorus, we likewise thereby discover that it is impossible for Hesperus to be anything other than Phosphorus.

As previously indicated, we do not want to put much emphasis on this kind of case. We think that any picture of the empirical component of modal epistemology as solely a matter of identity and distinctness would be highly impoverished; the rich modal content of science, according to our preferred form of modal naturalism, goes beyond logical consequences of identities. Nonetheless, where theoretical identities are discovered by science, they have modal consequences.

9.6 Summary

In this section we have supplemented our discussion of scientific discovery of possibility with a converse set of cases, in which some phenomenon is discovered to be impossible in virtue of information about its underlying nature which can be revealed by the progress of science. Superseded 'framework' theories such as classical mechanics encode their own necessities, and our best contemporary physics is rich in them. Both quantum theory and relativity theory, the pillars of modern physics, are naturally interpreted as imposing substantive non-trivial restrictions on metaphysical possibility, concerning allowed transitions in a quantum world and information transfer in a relativistic spacetime. Further cases of scientific discoveries of necessity flow from higher-level sciences also, in cases when the way in which the higher-level phenomena are realised by lower-level phenomena places constraints on the behaviour of the higher level which would not have been otherwise anticipated from the higher-level point of view.

10 The Virtues of Modal Naturalism

10.1 Putting the Pieces Together

Our case for modal naturalism has so far focused on specific cases from the history of science. In this section we consider some more general considerations which favour modal naturalism. We identify three respects in which we think modal naturalism improves our epistemic position with respect to the modal facts: it permits a direct link between model-based science and the epistemology of counterfactuals (Section 10.2), it attaches no epistemic weight to intuition, thereby avoiding the associated problems of cultural variation and historical unreliability (Section 10.3), and it provides traction on modal disagreement and modal error (Section 10.4). Putting these together, it seems that modal naturalism grounds a moderately optimistic attitude to modal epistemology; we can often obtain good evidence bearing on modal facts of interest through available evidential channels.

We believe that modal naturalism improves the overall epistemic outlook of modal epistemology. That is because it allows the epistemic credentials of modal inquiry to hang at least partly on the epistemic credentials of science – which are, by most accounts, comparably quite good.[30] Since naturalistic modal inquiry is constrained by science, it inherits some of the epistemic support that science enjoys – whether that's understood in terms of justification, warrant, confirmation, or whatever else – proportional to the degree of constraint. So the more robustly science epistemically constrains our view of the modal facts, the rosier the prospects of modal epistemology. For instance, if constraint takes the form of deductive implication, the resulting view of the modal facts is equally well-supported as the constraining science. By contrast, the more our modal claims depart ampliatively from the scientific evidence, the less support they inherit and the more epistemic risk is introduced. There is room for modal naturalists to disagree about which degrees of constraint, support, and risk are acceptable or best. The point is that naturalistic modal epistemology has comparatively good epistemic prospects, in virtue of having a well-sourced pipeline of epistemic support.

There is, we take it, pre-philosophical reason to think that humans do have extensive modal knowledge – difficult though this knowledge might seem to account for from a philosophical point of view. An account of modal epistemology which underwrites widespread modal knowledge is therefore more plausible, we think, than one on which modal knowledge is very hard to come by and the pragmatic usefulness of our practices of modal and counterfactual reasoning goes unexplained. Accordingly, the moderate epistemic optimism enabled by modal naturalism should be viewed as a point in its support.

10.2 Modal Naturalism and Scientific Modelling

In Sections 8 and 9 we discussed numerous examples from scientific progress in which revisions were made – rationally, we think – to prior modal beliefs. In these examples, science has led us to revise certain modal beliefs concerning possibility and impossibility. But modal epistemology is not limited to determining the modal status of propositions. There is also, we take it, an objective structure to the modal domain which can be captured in terms of counterfactual conditionals. In this section we accordingly turn to a different source of modal discovery in science: model-supported counterfactual and explanatory reasoning.

In Section 7 we discussed Williamson's account of the connection between scientific models and counterfactuals. We agree with Williamson that model-based reasoning in science is a key route to the acquisition of modal knowledge, a conclusion which we regard as providing support for modal naturalism. We

---

[30] Yet, of course, they remain far from optimal. Precisely how highly to rank the epistemic credentials of science is a matter of debate. Assessing those credentials should involve careful consideration of a variety of arguable bugs and features of the institution of science and of scientific theory, practice, and practitioners (see, e.g., Haack 2003).

will not dwell on Williamson's specific view any further – in particular, we will not try to assess which types of modal naturalism may or may not be part of Williamson's position. Our focus is on the general argumentative strategy Williamson deploys, which we take to complement our more specific case-based arguments in Sections 8 and 9.

It is commonplace in philosophy of science to assign a central role to models in contemporary science; these models are said to be the source of our best predictive accuracy, the seat of explanation (Woodward 2003), or even the literal content of scientific theories, as in the semantic view of theories associated with Suppes (1967) and van Fraassen (1980). It is through these models that we address counterfactual questions of our theories: if we want to know how a 4° temperature rise will affect the ice caps, then we look at a range of climate models in which temperature rises 4°, and if we want to predict the folding structure of a given protein – perhaps a novel molecule which has never previously been synthesised – we typically ask a machine-learning algorithm to explore the space of possible structural models for that protein and evaluate their properties.

Scientific models have modal content insofar as they include parameters taking a range of values, where these values may be interpreted as characterising alternative worldly possibilities. An overview of this general line of thought may be found in Grüne-Yanoff and Wirling (2021). The essentially modal content of scientific theories has been emphasised by a broad range of authors including Ladyman (2000), Ladyman and Ross (2007), French (2014), and Ismael (2017); a version is expressed pithily by Maudlin (2020). It is also a standard feature of dispositional essentialism (associated with authors such as Ellis 2001, Bird 2007, and Vetter 2015) to regard scientific theories as modally rich, with this modal content encoded in those theories' models.

Modal naturalism meshes very naturally with this use of models in science. The near-universal practice of constructing scientific models which are understood to have modal content is understood as part and parcel of the standard representational function of scientific theories. The job of science is to describe the facts, and since these facts include the modal facts then it is part of the function of science to describe these also. Modal naturalists understand the standard practices of observation and data-gathering, systematisation and theorisation, as generating evidence which bears on modal and non-modal facts alike. Identifying the chemical compound responsible for the orange colour of a carrot might support the non-modal hypothesis that actual root vegetables rich in that substance will be found to be orange, while simultaneously supporting the modal hypothesis that if a carrot plant were genetically engineered not to produce that substance, its roots would not be orange.

Modal naturalism says that it is through science that we discover facts about the space of genuine possibilities and about an objective counterfactual structure over that space. This account explains the widespread use of model-based reasoning in science for both predictive and explanatory purposes. While other accounts of modal epistemology may be able to provide accounts of the ubiquity of model-based reasoning in science, we submit that any such account will be unable to match the simplicity and directness of the modal naturalist account of the role of scientific models.

10.3 Intuitions, Disagreement, and Error

As we discussed in Section 4, we take reliance on intuitions as evidence in modal epistemology to be a serious theoretical cost. We derived a non-exhaustive list of desiderata, according to which a satisfactory modal epistemology should: (1) limit the role of intuitions (or, at least, dubious forms of intuition), (2) have relatively good traction on disagreement, and (3) have the resources to identify and account for modal error. We believe modal naturalism satisfies all three.

Perhaps one of the most significant virtues of modal naturalism is that it assigns no evidential role to intuition. To say that we assign no direct evidential role to intuition is not to guarantee the first-order metaphysical fruits of modal naturalism to be intuition-free. To give such a guarantee would be naive, since intuitions have a way of cropping up, often inconspicuously and sometimes, arguably, in scientific contexts (Devitt 2006; Tallant 2013; Rowbottom 2014). What it does mean is that we build no explicit or direct role for intuitions into our modal epistemology in the way that many rationalist frameworks do. Nor do we believe modal naturalism permits any back door through which intuitions can systematically sneak into first-order modal metaphysics, in the way that (we have argued) some modal empiricist frameworks do. We take this diminished role for intuition to likewise improve the epistemic outlook for modal naturalism relative to rival frameworks.

Moreover, by eschewing direct reliance on intuitions, modal naturalism avoids brute disagreement. In fact, it has relatively rich resources for resolving disagreement. Disagreements among modal naturalists concern things like the scientific facts, as well as their interpretation, application, and explanation. Far from simply stomping one's foot, there are things we can do to make headway on such matters. Disagreements regarding the data can be resolved by consulting scientists and scientific publications. Disagreements about matters of interpretation, application, and explanation are amenable to reasoned argumentation. For instance, we can compare the explanatory payoffs and deficiencies of particular theoretical interpretations, spell out ceteris paribus conditions for physical laws in order to clarify their application, or compare explanations with respect to various measures of explanatory power and theoretical virtue. Disagreement among modal naturalists is thus often tractable.

Finally, the cases of scientific discovery we have emphasised show that science is sometimes an effective means of identifying and debunking spurious modal intuitions. More generally, the modal naturalist has comparatively rich resources for explaining and guarding against modal error. The loci of error are similar to the loci of disagreement: we can err in understanding, interpreting, applying, and explaining the relevant science – or, indeed, in the science itself. Errors in the science itself might include perceptual errors, measurement errors, mathematical errors, or errors deriving from incomplete or otherwise faulty evidence. These sorts of errors are typically identifiable and correctable. As for understanding, interpreting, applying, and explaining the relevant science, some errors will be easily identifiable and correctable in the normal course of research dissemination. They might be factual errors, mathematical errors, or argumentative errors such as fallacies. Others will be less straightforwardly identified, but still subject to more or less well-reasoned argument than simple declarations of, for example, what one can or cannot conceive. Modal naturalism gets solid traction on modal error by attributing modal error to a variety of relatively familiar and transparent sources. We take modal naturalism's satisfaction of this desideratum to be a powerful point in its favour.

10.4 Summary

This section has surveyed some of the broader advantages of modal naturalism, in virtue of which we find it to be a comparatively attractive programme. Modal naturalism improves the epistemic prospects of modal inquiry by tethering it to science. It accounts for the universal scientific practice of extracting modal conclusions – especially counterfactual conclusions – from scientific models. Moreover, it assigns no direct evidential role to intuitions, which are epistemically worrisome in a number of respects. Relatively unencumbered by intuitions, the modal naturalist has rich resources for resolving disagreement and identifying and accounting for modal error. For these reasons, as well as its smooth treatment of the cases in Sections 8 and 9, we believe modal naturalism should be recognised not only as a distinctive modal epistemological framework but also as a highly plausible one.

11 Conclusion

In this Element, we have developed and defended an alternative to standard modal epistemologies that we have called *modal naturalism*. Modal naturalism is a programme – a family of views that can be formulated in different ways, with differing strengths – but at minimum it recognises that science is an especially important source of evidence concerning the modal facts. Characterising the nature of the view has required some nuance – nuance that we hope will be carried over fruitfully to further discussions in the epistemology of modality. In particular, we have taken care to correctly position modal naturalism with respect to entangled epistemological and metaphysical issues. We characterised modal naturalism as an epistemological view, because it concerns the path to modal knowledge and because we see it as directly competing with modal rationalism and modal empiricism (though not all formulations of it are strictly incompatible with them). Likewise, we have characterised the 'naturalism' in 'modal naturalism' as an epistemological form of naturalism, according to which the state of our best theorising in science places distinctive epistemic constraints on modal theorising. But modal naturalism also has immediate implications for the practice of modal metaphysics – at least, important aspects of it – such that modal naturalism can be understood as motivating naturalised modal metaphysics.

When setting up our discussion, we distinguished between core and extensional aspects of modal metaphysics. Core modal metaphysics comprises foundational matters and principles; extensional modal metaphysics comprises individual modal cases. Modal naturalism is an epistemology of the extensional aspects of modal metaphysics – it is a view about knowledge of the modal facts. While those with theoretical proclivities may favour a top-down approach in which foundational questions are settled first and the resulting theory is then applied to concrete cases, we think it fruitful to take a bottom-up approach and work from cases while being as theoretically neutral as possible (though we have discussed the limits of that neutrality and the ways in which different theoretical commitments will affect the interpretation and import of the cases).

We also distinguished between descriptive and prescriptive forms of modal naturalism. This distinction marked a difference between two different sorts of modal epistemological project. The first project seeks to identify actual, contingent conditions for modal knowledge in practice, among creatures suitably like us. Descriptive modal naturalism correspondingly says that the evidence by which we in fact gain our modal knowledge is scientific, or predominantly scientific, in character. The second project seeks to identify non-contingent conditions for any possible modal knowledge, for any possible epistemic agents. Prescriptive modal naturalism correspondingly says that scientific evidence is indispensable as a primary route to modal knowledge. Prescriptive modal naturalism is a natural fit with various necessitarian hypotheses in the metaphysics of modality, while descriptive modal naturalism remains more neutral on associated metaphysical questions.

One of the overarching goals of this Element was to flesh out what we take to be an overlooked and distinctive theoretical alternative within the epistemology of modality. We have highlighted the ways in which the modal epistemological terrain, as it has standardly been conceived, has been expanding, and we have aimed to contribute to its further expansion. As modal empiricists have recently emphasised, modal rationalism is not the only viable modal epistemology. Those who wish to acknowledge and account for modal knowledge need not, for lack of a better alternative, hang it directly on dubious forms of rational insight such as modal intuition. However, the addition of empiricism to the scene has not resulted in a totally clean or complete taxonomy. The differences between modal rationalism and modal empiricism do not always run as deep as proponents think, as we suggested when we raised the concern that some forms of modal empiricism may differ only cosmetically from their rationalist rivals. Nor do modal rationalism and empiricism exhaust the theoretical options before us, as shown by counterfactual accounts which rely on rational capacities but may also assign an important role to empirical background beliefs. There is clear dialectical space for a further view – modal naturalism – which is neither purely rationalist nor purely empiricist but which instead assigns a central role to the wildly successful epistemic enterprise that is science. We hope to see modal naturalism take its place as a serious theoretical option alongside modal rationalism, modal empiricism, and counterfactual accounts.

Indeed, the second overarching goal of this Element was to outline reasons for taking modal naturalism seriously. Not only does modal naturalism occupy a distinct position in theoretical space, but it is a well-evidenced and comparatively attractive position. Our examples demonstrating the relevance of science to modality speak against the historical assumption that modal naturalism would be a non-starter. The examples concerned scientific discoveries of possibilities and impossibilities, such as those relating to the conditions of life, the mass or size of certain types of bodies, physical reactions, speed of travel, the predictability of human actions, and so on. We outlined several considerable advantages that modal naturalism has over standard modal epistemologies: it accounts straightforwardly for the use of models in science, it improves the epistemic credentials of modal inquiry, it assigns no direct role to intuitions, it has greater resources for resolving modal disagreement, and it has greater traction on modal error. We therefore hope others will join us in regarding modal naturalism as a valuable addition to the theoretical landscape.

References

Andersen, H. (2017). 'Patterns, Information and Causation', *Journal of Philosophy* 114(11): 592–622.

Anderson, S., Yamagishi, N., and Karavia, V. (2002). 'Attentional Processes Link Perception and Action', *Proceedings of the Royal Society B: Biological Sciences* 269: 1225–1232.

Andow, J. (2016). 'Reliable but Not Home Free? What Framing Effects Mean for Moral Intuitions', *Philosophical Psychology* 6: 1–8.

Andrade, V. and Pereira, J. (1997). 'Gravitational Lorentz Force and the Description of the Gravitational Interaction', *Physical Review D* 56(8): 4689.

Armstrong, D. (1983). *What Is a Law of Nature?* Cambridge: Cambridge University Press.

Bealer, G. (1987). 'The Philosophical Limits of Scientific Essentialism', *Philosophical Perspectives* 1: 289–365.

Bealer, G. (2002). 'Modal Epistemology and the Rationalist Renaissance', in T. Gendler and J. Hawthorne (eds.) *Conceivability and Possibility.* Oxford: Oxford University Press, pp. 71–126.

Beebe, J. R. and Undercoffer, R. (2016). 'Individual and Cross-Cultural Differences in Semantic Intuitions: New Experimental Findings', *Journal of Cognition and Culture* 16(3–4): 322–357.

Bernhard, E., Recker, J., & Burton-Jones, A. (2013). 'Understanding the actualization of affordances: a study in the process modeling context', in M. Chau & R. Baskerville (eds.) *Proceedings of the 34th International Conference on Information Systems (ICIS 2013).* Association for Information Systems (AIS), pp. 1–11.

Biggs, S. (2011). 'Abduction and Modality', *Philosophy and Phenomenological Research* 83(2): 283–326.

Bird, A. (2001). 'Necessarily, Salt Dissolves in Water', *Analysis* 61(4): 267–274.

Bird, A. (2007). *Nature's Metaphysics: Laws and Properties.* Oxford: Oxford University Press.

Bird, A. (2022). *Knowing Science.* Oxford: Oxford University Press.

Blackburn, S. (1993). 'Morals and Modals', in *Essays in Quasi-Realism.* Oxford: Oxford University Press, pp. 52–74.

Boardman, S. and Schoonen, T. (2023). 'Epistemologists of Modality Wanted', *Synthese* 202(6): 1–20.

Bryant, A. (2020a). 'Keep the Chickens Cooped: The Epistemic Inadequacy of Free Range Metaphysics', *Synthese* 197: 1867–1887.

Bryant, A. (2020b). 'Naturalisms', *Think* 19(56): 35–50.

Bryant, A. (2021). 'Epistemic Infrastructure for a Scientific Metaphysics', *Grazer Philosophische Studien* 98(1): 27–49.

Bryant, A. (2022). 'The Supposed Spectre of Scientism', in M. Mizrahi (ed.) *For and against Scientism: Science, Methodology, and the Future of Philosophy.* Lanham: Rowman and Littlefield, pp. 47–74.

Bueno, O. and Shalkowski, S. (2014). 'Modalism and Theoretical Virtues: Toward an Epistemology of Modality', *Philosophical Studies* 172(3): 671–689.

Buller, D. (2012). 'Four Fallacies of Pop Evolutionary Psychology', *Scientific American Special Editions* 22(1S): 44–51.

Burge, T. (1993). Content Preservation, *Philosophical Review* 102 (4): 457–488.

Burge, T. (2003). 'Perceptual Entitlement', *Philosophy and Phenomenological Research* 67(3): 503–548.

Caiani, S. Z. (2014). 'Extending the Notion of Affordance', *Phenomenology and the Cognitive Sciences* 13(2): 275–293.

Callender, C. (2011). 'Philosophy of Science and Metaphysics', in S. French and J. Saatsi (eds.) *The Continuum Companion to the Philosophy of Science.* New York: Continuum, pp. 33–54.

Callender, C. (2017). *What Makes Time Special?* Oxford: Oxford University Press.

Cameron, R. (2010). 'The Grounds of Necessity', *Philosophy Compass* 5(4): 348–358.

Cameron, R. (2012). 'Why Lewis's Analysis of Modality Succeeds in Its Reductive Ambitions', *Philosophers' Imprint* 12(8): 1–21.

Chakravartty, A. (2013). 'On the Prospects of Naturalized Metaphysics', in D. Ross, J. Ladyman, and H. Kincaid (eds.) *Scientific Metaphysics.* Oxford: Oxford University Press, pp. 27–50.

Chakravartty, A. (2017). *Scientific Ontology: Integrating Naturalized Metaphysics and Voluntarist Epistemology.* New York: Oxford University Press.

Chalmers, D. (1996). *The Conscious Mind: In Search of a Fundamental Theory.* Oxford: Oxford University Press.

Chalmers, D. (2002). 'Does Conceivability Entail Possibility?', in T. Gendler and J. Hawthorne (eds.) *Conceivability and Possibility.* Oxford: Oxford University Press, pp. 145–200.

Chemero, A. (2003). 'An Outline of a Theory of Affordances', *Ecological Psychology* 15(2): 181–195.

Cowling, S. (2011). 'The Limits of Modality', *Philosophical Quarterly* 61-(244): 473–495.

Craighero, L., Fadiga, L., Umiltà, C. A., and Rizzolatti, G. (1996). 'Evidence for Visuomotor Priming Effect', *NeuroReport* 8(1): 347–349.

Cullen, S. (2010). 'Survey-Driven Romanticism', *Review of Philosophy and Psychology* 1(2): 275–296.

Demarest, H. (2016). 'The Universe Had One Chance', *Philosophy of Science* 83(2): 248–264.

Dennett, D. (1992). *Consciousness Explained*. New York: Little, Brown.

Deutsch, M. (2009). 'Experimental Philosophy and the Theory of Reference', *Mind and Language* 24: 445–466.

Devitt, M. (2006). 'Intuitions in Linguistics', *British Journal for the Philosophy of Science* 57(3): 481–513.

Devitt, M. (2011). 'Experimental Semantics', *Philosophy and Phenomenological Research* 82: 418–435.

Divers, J. (2009). 'Modal Commitments', in B. Hale and A. Hoffmann (eds.) *Modality: Metaphysics, Logic, and Epistemology*. Oxford: Oxford University Press, pp. 189–219.

Dohrn, D. (2020). 'Counterfactuals and Non-exceptionalism about Modal Knowledge', *Erkenntnis* 85(6): 1461–1483.

Dowe, P. (2000). *Physical Causation*. Cambridge: Cambridge University Press.

Drayson, Z. (2021). 'Naturalism and the Metaphysics of Perception', in H. Logue and L. Richardson (eds.) *Purpose and Procedure in Philosophy of Perception*. Oxford: Oxford University Press, pp. 215–233.

Edgington, D. (2004). 'Two Kinds of Possibility', *Aristotelian Society Supplementary* 78: 1–22.

Einstein, A. (1918). 'Letter to Max Born', reprinted in M. Born (ed.) *Albert Einstein – Hedwig und Max Born. Briefwechsel, 1916–1955*. Munich: Nymphenburger (1969), pp. 6–8.

Ellis, B. (2001). *Scientific Essentialism*. Cambridge: Cambridge University Press.

Emery, N. (2023). *Naturalism beyond the Limits of Science: How Scientific Methodology Can and Should Shape Philosophical Theorizing*. Oxford: Oxford University Press.

Evans, S., Pearce, K., Vitak, J., and Treem, J. (2016). 'Explicating Affordances: A Conceptual Framework for Understanding Affordances in Communication Research', *Journal of Computer-Mediated Communication* 22(1): 35–52.

Fischer, B. (2015). 'Theory Selection in Modal Epistemology', *American Philosophical Quarterly* 52(4): 381–395.

Fischer, B. (2016). 'A Theory-Based Epistemology of Modality', *Canadian Journal of Philosophy* 46: 228–247.

Fischer, B. (2017). *Modal Justification via Theories*. Cham: Springer.

Fischer, B. and Leon, F. (eds.) (2017). *Modal Epistemology after Rationalism*. Dordrecht: Springer.

French, S. (2014). *The Structure of the World: Metaphysics and Representation*. Oxford: Oxford University Press.

French, S. and McKenzie, K. (2012). 'Thinking Outside the Toolbox: Towards a More Productive Engagement between Metaphysics and Philosophy of Physics', *European Journal of Analytic Philosophy* 8(1): 42–59.

French, S. and Murphy, A. (2023). 'The Value of Surprise in Science', *Erkenntnis* 88(4): 1447–1466.

Fricke, B. and Soff, G. (1977). 'Dirac-Fock-Slater Calculations for the Elements Z = 100, Fermium, to Z = 173', *Atomic Data and Nuclear Data Tables* 19(1): 83–95.

Fromm, J., Mirbabaie, M., and Stieglitz, S. (2020). 'A Systematic Review of Empirical Affordance Studies: Recommendations for Affordance Research in Information Systems', *ECIS 2020 Research-in-Progress Papers* 42.

Galileo (1632/2023). *Dialogue Concerning the Two Chief World Systems*. University of California Press.

Geirsson, H. (2005). 'Conceivability and Defeasible Modal Justification', *Philosophical Studies* 122(3): 279–304.

Gibson, J. (1979). *The Ecological Approach to Visual Perception*. Boston: Houghton Mifflin.

Goswick, D. (2015). 'Why Being Necessary Really Is Not the Same as Being Not Possibly Not', *Acta Analytica* 30(3): 267–274.

Grèzes, J. and Decety, J. (2002). 'Does Visual Perception of Object Afford Action? Evidence from a Neuroimaging Study', *Neuropsychologia* 40(2): 212–222.

Grüne-Yanoff, T. and Wirling, Y. (2021). 'The Epistemology of Modal Modelling', *Philosophy Compass*, 16(10): e12775.

Guan, C. and Firestone, C. (2020). 'Seeing What's Possible: Disconnected Visual Parts Are Confused for Their Potential Wholes', *Journal of Experimental Psychology: General* 149(3): 590–598.

Guan, C., Schwitzgebel, D., Hafri, A., and Firestone, C. (2020). 'Possible Objects Count: Perceived Numerosity Is Altered by Representations of Possibility', *Journal of Vision* 20(11): 847.

Haack, S. (2003). *Defending Science – within Reason: Between Scientism and Cynicism*. Amherst: Prometheus Books.

Haldane, J. B. (1926). 'On Being the Right Size', *The Harper's Monthly* March, 424–427.

Hale, B. (2002). 'Knowledge of Possibility and of Necessity', *Proceedings of the Aristotelian Society* 103(1): 1–20.

Hanrahan, R. R. (2009). 'Consciousness and Modal Empiricism', *Philosophia* 37: 281–306.

Hansson, S. O. (2019). 'Farmers' Experiments and Scientific Methodology', *European Journal for the Philosophy of Science* 9(3): 1–23.

Heras-Escribano, M. (2019). *The Philosophy of Affordances*. Cham: Palgrave Macmillan.

Hill, C. S. (2006). 'Modality, Modal Epistemology, and the Metaphysics of Consciousness', in S. Nichols (ed.) *The Architecture of the Imagination: New Essays on Pretense, Possibility, and Fiction*. Oxford: Oxford University Press, pp. 205–235.

Hirvonen, I., Koskinen, R., and Pättiniemi, I. (2021). 'Modal Inferences in Science: A Tale of Two Epistemologies', *Synthese* 199(5–6): 13823–13843.

Hume, D. (2000/1739). *A Treatise of Human Nature* (Oxford Philosophical Texts). Eds. D. Norton and M. Norton. Oxford: Oxford University Press.

Ichikawa, J., Maitra, I., and Weatherson, B. (2012). 'In Defense of a Kripkean Dogma', *Philosophy and Phenomenological Research* 85: 56–68.

Ismael, J. (2017). 'An Empiricist's Guide to Objective Modality', in Z. Yudall and M. Slater (eds.) *Metaphysics and the Philosophy of Science*. Oxford: Oxford University Press, pp. 109–125.

Jenkins, C. (2010). 'Concepts, Experience and Modal Knowledge', *Philosophical Perspectives* 24: 255–279.

Kant, I. (1781/1998). *Kritik der reinen Vernunft*. Eds. G. Mohr and M. Willaschek. Berlin: Akademie Verlag.

Kaplan, J. (2002). 'Historical Evidence and Human Adaptations', *Philosophy of Science* 69(S3): S294–S304.

Kauppinen, A. (2007). 'The Rise and Fall of Experimental Philosophy', *Philosophical Explorations* 10(2): 95–118.

Knobe, J. (2019). 'Philosophical Intuitions Are Surprisingly Robust across Demographic Differences', *Epistemology and Philosophy of Science* 56(2): 29–36.

Knox, E. (2011). 'Newton–Cartan Theory and Teleparallel Gravity: The Force of a Formulation', *Studies in History and Philosophy of Modern Physics* 42: 264–275.

Kriegel, U. (2013). 'The Epistemological Challenge of Revisionary Metaphysics', *Philosophers' Imprint* 13(12): 1–30.

Kripke, S. (1980). *Naming and Necessity*. Cambridge, MA: Harvard University Press.

Kroedel, T. (2012). 'Counterfactuals and the Epistemology of Modality', *Philosophers' Imprint* 12(12): 1–14.

Kroedel, T. (2017). 'Modal Knowledge, Evolution, and Counterfactuals', in B. Fischer and F. Leon (eds.) *Modal Epistemology after Rationalism*. Dordrecht: Synthese Library, pp. 179–196.

Ladyman, J. (2000). 'What's Really Wrong with Constructive Empiricism?: van Fraassen and the Metaphysics of Modality', *The British Journal for the Philosophy of Science* 51(2): 837–856.

Ladyman, J. and Ross, D. with Spurrett, D. and Collier, J. (2007). *Every Thing Must Go: Metaphysics Naturalized*. Oxford: Oxford University Press.

Lam, B. (2010). 'Are Cantonese Speakers Really Descriptivists? Revisiting Cross-Cultural Semantics', *Cognition* 115(2): 320–332.

Lange, M. (2005). 'A Counterfactual Analysis of the Concepts of Logical Truth and Necessity', *Philosophical Studies* 125: 277–303.

Lange, M. (2009). *Laws and Lawmakers: Science, Metaphysics and the Laws of Nature*. Oxford: Oxford University Press.

Leeds, S. (2007). 'Physical and Metaphysical Necessity', *Pacific Philosophical Quarterly* 88(4): 458–485.

Lewis, D. (1986). 'Introduction', in *Philosophical Papers Vol. 2*. Oxford: Blackwell, pp. ix–xvii.

Li, J., Longgen, L., Chalmers, E., and Snedeker, J. (2018). 'What Is in a Name?: The Development of Cross-Cultural Differences in Referential Intuitions', *Cognition* 171: 108–111.

Libet, B., Gleason, C., Wright, E., and Pearl, D. (1983). 'Time of Conscious Intention to Act in Relation to Onset of Cerebral Activity (Readiness-Potential): The Unconscious Initiation of a Freely Voluntary Act', *Brain* 106(3): 623–642.

Linnemann, N. (2020). 'On Metaphysically Necessary Laws from Physics', *European Journal for Philosophy of Science* 10(2): 1–13.

Loewer, B. (2020). 'The Mentaculus Vision', in V. Allori (ed.) *Statistical Mechanics and Scientific Explanation: Determinism, Indeterminism and Laws of Nature*. Singapore: World Scientific, pp. 3–29.

Lowe, E. J. (1998). *The Possibility of Metaphysics: Substance, Identity, and Time*. Oxford: Clarendon Press.

Machery, E., Mallon, R., Nichols, S., Stich, S. (2004). 'Semantics, Cross-Cultural Style', *Cognition* 92(3): B1–B12.

Malament, D. (1986). 'Newtonian Gravity, Limits, and the Geometry of Space', in R. Colodny (ed.) *From Quarks to Quasars: Philosophical Problems of Modern Physics*. Pittsburgh: University of Pittsburgh Press, pp. 181–201.

Mallozzi, A. (2020). 'Superexplanations for Counterfactual Knowledge', *Philosophical Studies* 178: 1315–1337.

Mallozzi, A. (2021). 'Putting Modal Metaphysics First', *Synthese* 198(Suppl 8): 1937–1956.

Mallozzi, A., Vaidya, A., and Wallner, M. (2023). 'The Epistemology of Modality', in E. Zalta (ed.) *The Stanford Encyclopedia of Philosophy*. https://plato.stanford.edu/archives/sum2024/entries/modality-epistemology/.

Malmgren, A. (2006). 'Is There a Priori Knowledge by Testimony?', *Philosophical Review* 115(2): 199–241.

Mandelbaum, E. (2018). 'Seeing and Conceptualizing: Modularity and the Shallow Contents of Perception', *Philosophy and Phenomenological Research* 97(2): 267–283.

Martí, G. (2009). 'Against Semantic Multi-culturalism', *Analysis* 69: 42–48.

Maudlin, T. (2007). *The Metaphysics within Physics*. Oxford: Oxford University Press.

Maudlin, T. (2020). 'A Modal Free Lunch', *Foundations of Physics* 50(6): 522–529.

McKenzie, K. (2017). 'Relativities of Fundamentality', *Studies in History and Philosophy of Modern Physics* 59: 89–99.

Mele, A. (2008). *Free Will and Luck*. Oxford: Oxford University Press.

Menzies, P. (1998). 'Possibility and Conceivability: A Response-Dependent Account of Their Connections', in R. Casati (ed.) *European Review of Philosophy, Volume 3: Response-Dependence*. Stanford: CSLI, pp. 255–277.

Minkowski, H. (1952). 'Space and Time', in H. A. Lorentz, A. Einstein, H. Minkowski, and H. Weyl (eds.) *The Principle of Relativity: A Collection of Original Memoirs on the Special and General Theory of Relativity*. New York: Dover, pp. 75–91.

Morganti, M. & Tahko, T. (2017). 'Moderately Naturalistic Metaphysics', *Synthese* 194(7): 2557–2580.

Mumford, S. & Tugby, M. (2013). 'Introduction', in Mumford and Tugby (eds.) *Metaphysics and Science*. Oxford: Oxford University Press, pp. 3–28.

Nichols, S., Stich, S., and Weinberg, J. (2003). 'Metaskepticism: Meditations in Ethnoepistemology', in S. Luper (ed.) *The Skeptics*. Burlington: Ashgate, pp. 227–247.

Nolan, D. (2017). 'Naturalised Modal Epistemology', in B. Fischer and F. Leon (eds.) *Modal Epistemology after Rationalism*. Dordrecht: Springer, pp. 7–27.

Panksepp, J. and Panksepp, J. (2000). 'Historical Evidence and Human Adaptations', *Evolution and Cognition* 6(2): 108–131.

Papineau, D. (2020). 'Naturalism', in E. N. Zalta and U. Nodelman (eds.) *The Stanford Encyclopedia of Philosophy*. https://plato.stanford.edu/archives/sum2020/entries/naturalism/.

Paul, L. A. (2012). 'Metaphysics as Modeling: The Handmaiden's Tale', *Philosophical Studies* 160(1): 1–29.

Peacocke, C. (1999). *Being Known*. Oxford: Oxford University Press.

Price, H. (1996). *Time's Arrow and Archimedes' Point: New Directions for the Physics of Time*. New York: Oxford University Press.

Price, H. (2004). 'Models and Modals', in D. Gillies (ed.) *Laws and Models in Science*. London: King's College, pp. 49–69.

Priest, G. (1987). *In Contradiction: a Study of the Transconsistent*. New York: Oxford University Press.

Quine, W. V. O. (1953a). 'Reference and Modality', in *From a Logical Point of View*. Cambridge, MA: Harvard University Press, pp. 139–159.

Quine, W. V. O. (1953b). 'Three Grades of Modal Involvement', *Proceedings of the XIth International Congress of Philosophy* 14: 65–81, reprinted in *The Ways of Paradox and Other Essays* (1976). New York: Random House, pp. 156–174.

Rayo, A. (2013). *The Construction of Logical Space*. Oxford: Oxford University Press.

Roca-Royes, S. (2007). 'Mind-Independence and Modal Empiricism', in C. Penco, M. Vignolo, V. Ottonelli, C. Amoretti (eds.) *4th Latin Meeting in Analytic Philosophy, CEUR-WS Proceedings*. Genoa: University of Genoa, pp. 117–135.

Roca-Royes, S. (2011). 'Modal Knowledge and Counterfactual Knowledge', *Logique et Analyse* 54: 537–552.

Roca-Royes, S. (2017). 'Similarity and Possibility: An Epistemology of de re Possibility for Concrete Entities', in B. Fischer and F. Leon (eds.) *Modal Epistemology After Rationalism*. Synthese Library, vol 378. Springer, Cham.

Roca-Royes, S. (2018). 'Rethinking the Epistemology of Modality for Abstracta', in I. Fred and J. Leech (eds.) *Being Necessary: Themes of Ontology and Modality from the Work of Bob Hale*. Oxford: Oxford University Press, pp. 245–265.

Rowbottom, D. P. (2014). 'Intuitions in Science: Thought Experiments as Argument Pumps', in A. R. Booth and D. P. Rowbottom (eds.) *Intuitions*. Oxford: Oxford University Press, pp. 119–134.

Scarantino, A. (2003). 'Affordances Explained', *Philosophy of Science* 70(5): 949–961.

Schaffer, J. and Ismael, J. (2020). 'Quantum Holism: Nonseparability as Common Ground', *Synthese* 197: 4131–4160.

Schwitzgebel, E. and Cushman, F. (2012). 'Expertise in Moral Reasoning? Order Effects on Moral Judgment in Professional Philosophers and Non-philosophers', *Mind and Language* 27(2): 135–153.

Schelling, T. C. (1971). 'Dynamic Models of Segregation', *Journal of Mathematical Sociology* 1: 143–186.

Shoemaker, S. (1980). 'Causality and Properties', in P. van Inwagen (ed.) *Time and Cause*. D. Reidel. pp. 109–35.

Shtulman, A. and Harrington, K. (2016). 'Tensions between Science and Intuition across the Lifespan', *Topics in Cognitive Science* 8: 118–137.

Sidelle, A. (2010). 'Modality and Objects', *The Philosophical Quarterly* 60-(238): 109–125.

Siegel, S. (2014). 'Affordances and the Contents of Perception', in B. Brogaard (ed.) *Does Perception Have Content?* Oxford: Oxford University Press, pp. 39–76.

Sloman, A. (1996). 'Actual Possibilities', in L. Aiello and S. Shapiro (eds.) *Principles of Knowledge Representation and Reasoning: Proc. 5th Int. Conf. (KR '96)*. Boston: Morgan Kaufmann, pp. 627–638.

Stoffregen, T. A. (2003). 'Affordances as Properties of the Animal-Environment', *Ecological Psychology* 15(2): 115–134.

Strohminger, M. (2015). 'Perceptual Knowledge of Nonactual Possibilities', *Philosophical Perspectives* 29: 363–375.

Suppes, P. (1967). 'What Is a Scientific Theory?', in S. Morgenbesser (ed.) *Philosophy of Science Today*. New York: Basic Books, pp. 55–67.

Susskind, L. (2006). *The Cosmic Landscape: String Theory and the Illusion of Cosmic Design*. New York: Little, Brown.

Swain, S., Alexander, J., and Weinberg, J. (2008). 'The Instability of Philosophical Intuitions: Running Hot and Cold on Truetemp', *Philosophy and Phenomenological Research* 76(1): 138–155.

Swoyer, C. (1982). 'The Nature of Natural Laws'. *Australasian Journal of Philosophy* 60 (3).

Sytsma, J., and Livengood, J. (2011). 'A New Perspective Concerning Experiments on Semantic Intuitions', *Australasian Journal of Philosophy* 89: 315–332.

Tahko, T. (2017). 'Empirically-Informed Modal Rationalism', in B. Fischer and F. Leon (eds.) *Modal Epistemology after Rationalism*. Cham: Springer, pp. 29–45.

Tahko, T. (2012). 'Counterfactuals and Modal Epistemology', *Grazer Philosophische Studien* 86 (1): 93–115.

Tallant, J. (2013). 'Intuitions in Physics', *Synthese* 190(15): 2959–2980.

Teller, P. (1986). 'Relational Holism and Quantum Mechanics', *The British Journal for the Philosophy of Science* 37(1): 71–81.

Thomasson, A. (2020). *Norms and Necessity*. Oxford: Oxford University Press.

Titelbaum, M. (2013). *Quitting Certainties: A Bayesian Framework for Modeling Degrees of Belief*. Oxford: Oxford University Press.

Tucker, M. and Ellis, R. (1998). 'On the Relations between Seen Objects and Components of Potential Actions', *Journal of Experimental Psychology: Human Perception and Performance* 24(3): 830–846.

Turvey, M. T., Shaw, R. E., Reed, E. S., Mace, W. M. (1981). 'Ecological Laws of Perceiving and Acting: In Reply to Fodor and Pylyshyn', *Cognition* 9(3): 237–304.

Van Fraassen, B. (1977). 'The Only Necessity Is Verbal Necessity', *Journal of Philosophy* 74(2): 71–85.

Van Fraassen, B. (1980). *The Scientific Image*. Oxford: Oxford University Press.

Van Inwagen, P. (1998). 'Modal Epistemology', *Philosophical Studies* 92: 67–84.

Verreault-Julien, P. (2019). 'How Could Models Possibly Provide How-Possibly Explanations?', *Studies in the History and Philosophy of Science Part A* 73: 22–33.

Vetter, B. (2015). *Potentiality: From Dispositions to Modality*. Oxford: Oxford University Press.

Weinberg, J., Nichols, S., and Stich, S. (2001). 'Normativity and Epistemic Intuitions', *Philosophical Topics* 29(1–2): 429–460.

Wheatley, T. and Haidt, J. (2005). 'Hypnotic Disgust Makes Moral Judgments More Severe', *Psychological Science* 16(10): 780–784.

Williamson, T. (2007). 'Knowledge of Metaphysical Modality', in *The Philosophy of Philosophy*. Malden: Blackwell, pp. 134–179.

Williamson, T. (2016). 'Modal Science', *Canadian Journal of Philosophy* 46 (4–5): 453–492.

Wilson, A. (2013). 'Schaffer on Laws of Nature', *Philosophical Studies* 164(3): 654–667.

Wilson, A. (2020). *The Nature of Contingency: Quantum Physics as Modal Realism*. Oxford: Oxford University Press.

Wilson, A. (Forthcoming). 'Four Grades of Modal Naturalism', to appear in *Proceedings of the Aristotelian Society*.

Wirling, Y. (2020). 'Non-uniformism about the Epistemology of Modality: Strong and Weak', *Analytic Philosophy* 61(2): 152–173.

Wirling, Y. (2022). 'Extending Similarity-Based Epistemology of Modality with Models', *Ergo* 8: 45.

Withagen, R. and van Wermeskerken, M. (2010). 'The Role of Affordances in the Evolutionary Process Reconsidered: A Niche Construction Perspective', *Theory & Psychology* 20(4): 489–510.

Wolff, J. (2013). 'Are Conservation Laws Metaphysically Necessary', *Philosophy of Science* 80(5): 898–906.

Woodward, J. (2003). *Making Things Happen: A Theory of Causal Explanation*. Oxford: Oxford University Press.

Woolfolk, R. (2013). 'Experimental Philosophy: A Methodological Critique', *Metaphilosophy* 44 (1–2): 79–87.

Worley, S. (2003). 'Conceivability, Possibility and Physicalism', *Analysis* 63: 15–23.

Yablo, S. (1993). 'Is Conceivability a Guide to Possibility?', *Philosophy and Phenomenological Research* 53(1): 1–42.

Yli-Vakkuri, J. (2013). 'Modal Skepticism and Counterfactual Knowledge', *Philosophical Studies* 162(3): 605–623.

Acknowledgements

The authors would like to thank the anonymous reviewers of this Element for their time and for their invaluable feedback.

Amanda Bryant would like to thank Yuval Abrams, Gary Ostertag, as well as Christian Nimtz and the attendees of the workshop *Directions in the Epistemology of Modality* at the University of Stirling for their comments on a very early version of some of the material in this book.

Alastair Wilson would like to thank all the members of the FraMEPhys research group, Sam Baron, Nina Emery, Nicholas Jones, Kristie Miller, Daniel Nolan, Sonia Roca Royes, Scott Sturgeon, Miranda Rose, Barbara Vetter, and audiences at Bristol, Stirling, Geneva, ACU, Sydney, Brisbane, Leeds, and the Aristotelian Society.

This work forms part of the project A Framework for Metaphysical Explanation in Physics (FraMEPhys), which received funding from the European Research Council (ERC) under the European Union's Horizon 2020 research and innovation programme (grant agreement no. 757295). Funding for Alastair Wilson was also provided by the Australian Research Council (grant agreement no. DP180100105).

Cambridge Elements

Metaphysics

Tuomas E. Tahko
University of Bristol

Tuomas E. Tahko is Professor of Metaphysics of Science at the University of Bristol, UK. Tahko specialises in contemporary analytic metaphysics, with an emphasis on methodological and epistemic issues: 'meta-metaphysics'. He also works at the interface of metaphysics and philosophy of science: 'metaphysics of science'. Tahko is the author of *Unity of Science* (Cambridge University Press, 2021, *Elements in Philosophy of Science*), *An Introduction to Metametaphysics* (Cambridge University Press, 2015), and editor of *Contemporary Aristotelian Metaphysics* (Cambridge University Press, 2012).

About the Series

This highly accessible series of Elements provides brief but comprehensive introductions to the most central topics in metaphysics. Many of the Elements also go into considerable depth, so the series will appeal to both students and academics. Some Elements bridge the gaps between metaphysics, philosophy of science, and epistemology.

Cambridge Elements ☰

Metaphysics

Elements in the Series

Printed in the United States
by Baker & Taylor Publisher Services